Gregg College Typing

Series Six

Basic

Scot Ober, Ph.D.
Professor, Department of
Business Education and
Office Administration
Ball State University
Muncie, Indiana

Robert N. Hanson, Ed.D.
Professor, Department of
Office Administration and
Business Education
Northern Michigan University
Marquette, Michigan

Alan C. Lloyd, Ph.D.
Former Director,
Employment Testing
The Olsten Corporation
Westbury, New York

Robert P. Poland, Ph.D.
Professor, Business and
Distributive Education
Michigan State University
East Lansing, Michigan

Albert D. Rossetti, Ed.D.
Professor, Department of
Business Education and Office
Systems Administration
Montclair State College
Montclair, New Jersey

Fred E. Winger, Ed.D.
Former Professor, Office
Administration and
Business Education
Oregon State University
Corvallis, Oregon

GLENCOE

Macmillan/McGraw-Hill

New York, New York   Columbus, Ohio   Mission Hills, California   Peoria, Illinois

Gregg College Typing, Series Six
Basic

Imprint 1994
Copyright © 1989 by the Glencoe Division of Macmillan/McGraw-Hill School
Publishing Company. All rights reserved. Copyright © 1989, 1984, 1979, 1970,
1964, 1957 by McGraw-Hill, Inc. All rights reserved. Printed in the United States
of America. Except as permitted under the United States Copyright Act of 1976,
no part of this publication may be reproduced or distributed in any form or by any
means, or stored in a database or retrieval system, without the prior written permission of the publisher.

The text portion of this publication is published simultaneously as part of the
works entitled *Gregg Typing for Colleges, Intensive Course* and *Gregg Typing for
Colleges, Complete Course.*

Send all inquiries to: Glencoe Division, Macmillan/McGraw-Hill, 936 Eastwind
Drive, Westerville, Ohio 43081.

11 12 13 14 15   RRW   00 99 98 97 96 95 94

ISBN 0-07-038393-6

Contents

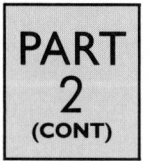

Index

TIMED WRITINGS

1-Minute		2-Minute	
Page	Words	Page	Words
5	10	18	38
6	12	20	40
8	13	21	42
9	14	23	44
11	15	25	46
12	16	27	48
14	17	28	50
15	18	30	52
17	19	31	54
		33	56

3-Minute		12-Second Sprints
Page	Words	Page
40	84	24
44	87	40
47	90	46
52	93	56
56	96	
61	99	
65	102	
69	105	
73	105	
77	108	
84	108	
93	108	
98	114	
102	114	
106	117	
110	117	
114	120	
118	120	
122	120	

Preface

Gregg College Typing, Series Six is a multicomponent instructional system designed to give the student and the instructor a high degree of flexibility and a high degree of success in meeting their respective goals. To facilitate the choice and use of materials, the core components of this teaching-learning system are available in either a kit format or a book format. The *Keyboarding, Second Edition* text is also available for the development of touch inputting skills for use on computer keyboards.

THE KIT FORMAT

Gregg College Typing, Series Six gives the student and the instructor the opportunity to obtain a complete kit of materials for each of the three semesters in the typing curriculum generally offered by colleges. Each of the kits, which are briefly described below, contains a softcover textbook, a pad of workbook materials, and a cardboard easel for use as a copyholder.

The text in each kit contains instructional materials for 60 lessons, each 45–50 minutes long. Each workbook—called a *Workguide*—provides a technique evaluation form; learning guides, letterheads and other stationery for use in completing the production jobs, placement guides, and materials for improving students' language-arts skills.

Kit 1: Basic. This kit provides the text and Workguide materials for Lessons 1 through 60. Since this kit is designed for the beginning student, its major objectives are to develop touch control of the keyboard and proper typing techniques, build basic speed and accuracy skills, and provide practice in applying those basic skills to the production of letters, reports, tables, memos, forms, and other kinds of personal, personal-business, and business communications.

Kit 2: Intermediate. This kit includes the text and Workguide materials for Lessons 61 through 120. This second-semester course continues the development of basic typing skills and emphasizes the production of various kinds of business correspondence, reports, tabulations, and forms from unarranged and rough-draft copy sources.

Kit 3: Advanced. This kit, which covers Lessons 121 through 180, is designed for the third semester. After a brief review of basic production techniques, each unit in this kit places the student in a different office situation where the emphasis is on such important modern office skills as editing, decision making, abstracting information, setting priorities, work flow, following directions, and working under pressure and with interruptions.

Format Guides. A pad of self-check keys is available for each of the three kits to enable students to check the correct format of all typed material.

THE BOOK FORMAT

For the convenience of those who wish to obtain the core instructional materials in separate volumes, the Gregg College Typing, Series Six system offers the following hardcover textbooks, workbooks, and self-check keys. In each instance, the content of the *Gregg College Typing* components is identical with that of the corresponding part or parts in the kit format.

Textbooks. *Gregg College Typing, Intensive Course* contains Lessons 1 through 120. The content and objectives of this two-semester hardcover text exactly match the content and objectives of the softcover textbooks in the *Basic* and *Intermediate* kits.

Gregg College Typing, Complete Course contains the text materials for Lessons 1 through 180. Thus it combines in one hardcover volume all the lessons contained in the three softcover textbooks included in the three kits.

Workbooks. The *Workguide* for each semester's work is available separately for use with the *Intensive* and *Complete* hardcover texts. These three workbooks are identical in content and purpose with those in the kits.

Format Guides. These self-check keys are also available for use with the *Intensive* and *Complete* hardcover texts.

SUPPORTING MATERIALS

The Gregg College Typing, Series Six system includes the following additional components for use with either Kit 1: Basic or the hardcover texts.

Recordings. The *Instructional Recordings for Lessons 1–60* consist of 30 cassettes (60 lessons) that provide the instructions for keyboard presentation, skillbuilding practice, introduction to production typing (letters, reports, forms, and tabulations), and timed writings for the entire first semester. The recordings free the instructor to work with the students individually to develop proper typing techniques. There is also a set of 12 cassettes (24 lessons) entitled *Keyboard Presentation Tapes* designed for use with the first 25 lessons only.

Progress Folder. The folder provides a lesson-by-lesson guide to the text activities, performance goals, and related instructional recordings and software for Lessons 1 through 60.

Instructor's Materials. The special materials provided for the instructor can be used with either the Gregg College Typing, Series Six kits or the hardcover texts. These materials include special Instructor's Editions of each of the three semesters. Also available are keys to the drills and production exercises for each semester and a manual of teaching suggestions.

Computer Software. Two microcomputer software programs are correlated directly with the textbooks for those classes using computers rather than typewriters:

1. The Keyboarding software provides instruction and practice on the alphabet, number, symbol, and 10-key number pad keys, as well as the basics of word processing including centering, underscoring, insert and delete functions, formatting, and so on.

2. The Skill Measurement Timings software provides unlimited opportunity for practice; administers and scores all Skill Measurement and test timings; scores the timings and highlights errors; reports speed and accuracy scores; and maintains complete records.

ACKNOWLEDGMENTS

We wish to express our appreciation to all the instructors and students who have used the previous editions and who have contributed much to this Sixth Edition.

The Authors

STANDARD FORMAT FOR LETTERS

Line length: 6-inch (60 pica/70 elite)
Style: modified-block
Paper: letterhead (business); plain (personal-business)
Paragraphs: blocked
Spacing: single
Date: line 15

ZIP Code: 1 space after state abbreviation
Punctuation: colon after salutation; comma after complimentary closing
Enumerations: numbers at left margin; turnover lines indented 4 spaces
Personal-business letter: no reference initials; return address in closing lines

---

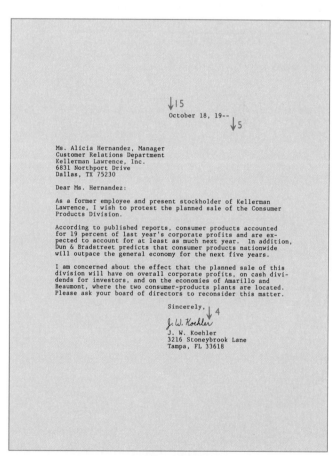

Employment Assistance Corporation
5133 Glentree Drive | San Jose, CA 95129

↓15
October 18, 19-- ↓5

Mr. James J. Novotny
Director of Human Resources
The Mitchell Company
7042 East Wesley Avenue
Denver, CO 80224-2536

Dear Mr. Novotny:

We would be happy to explore with you the possibility of our developing and validating an employment test for applicants for the position of assembler at your two plants. As shown in the enclosed brochure, we have developed many such tests for other companies during the ten years that our firm has been involved in employee testing.

On the basis of our preliminary discussions, the two main legal constraints we must be concerned with are as follows:

1. The test must accurately and reliably predict success on
4→ the job if it is to be used to make hiring decisions.

2. The test must not exclude a greater number of minority members than nonminority members.

I am asking Jeffrey Munter, one of our testing specialists, to call to set up an appointment with your personnel staff to explore this matter further. We look forward to serving you.

Sincerely, ↓4

Eleanor Wainwright
Eleanor Wainwright
Marketing Manager ↓2

dco
Enclosure
c: Jeffrey Munter

BUSINESS LETTER (Modified-Block Style)

↓15
October 18, 19-- ↓5

Ms. Alicia Hernandez, Manager
Customer Relations Department
Kellerman Lawrence, Inc.
6831 Northport Drive
Dallas, TX 75230

Dear Ms. Hernandez:

As a former employee and present stockholder of Kellerman Lawrence, I wish to protest the planned sale of the Consumer Products Division.

According to published reports, consumer products accounted for 19 percent of last year's corporate profits and are expected to account for at least as much next year. In addition, Dun & Bradstreet predicts that consumer products nationwide will outpace the general economy for the next five years.

I am concerned about the effect that the planned sale of this division will have on overall corporate profits, on cash dividends for investors, and on the economies of Amarillo and Beaumont, where the two consumer-products plants are located. Please ask your board of directors to reconsider this matter.

Sincerely, ↓4

J. W. Koehler
J. W. Koehler
3216 Stoneybrook Lane
Tampa, FL 33618

PERSONAL-BUSINESS LETTER (Modified-Block Style)

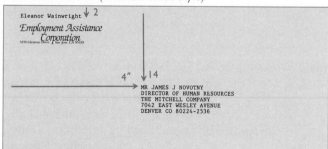

Eleanor Wainwright ↓2
Employment Assistance Corporation
5133 Glentree Drive | San Jose, CA 95129

4" ↓14
MR JAMES J NOVOTNY
DIRECTOR OF HUMAN RESOURCES
THE MITCHELL COMPANY
7042 EAST WESLEY AVENUE
DENVER CO 80224-2536

LARGE BUSINESS ENVELOPE (No. 10)

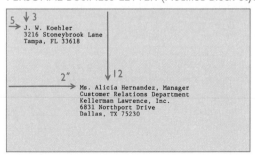

5 ↓3
J. W. Koehler
3216 Stoneybrook Lane
Tampa, FL 33618

2" ↓12
Ms. Alicia Hernandez, Manager
Customer Relations Department
Kellerman Lawrence, Inc.
6831 Northport Drive
Dallas, TX 75230

SMALL PLAIN ENVELOPE (No. 6¾)

STANDARD FORMAT FOR MEMOS

Line length: 6-inch (60 pica/70 elite)
Paragraphs: blocked
Spacing: single
Paper: printed form, plain paper, or letterhead
Top margin: 2 inches (full sheet);
　　　　　　　1 inch (half sheet)
Writer's initials: optional; typed a double space below
　　　　　　　the body beginning at the center point

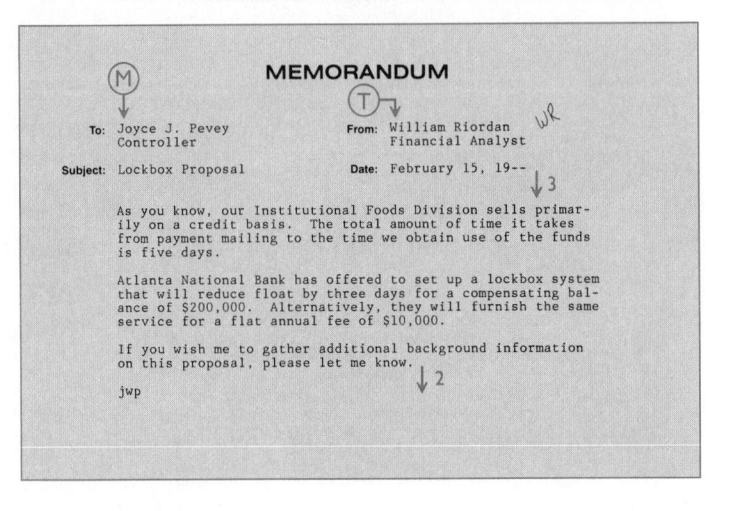

INTEROFFICE MEMORANDUM (Printed Form—Half Sheet)

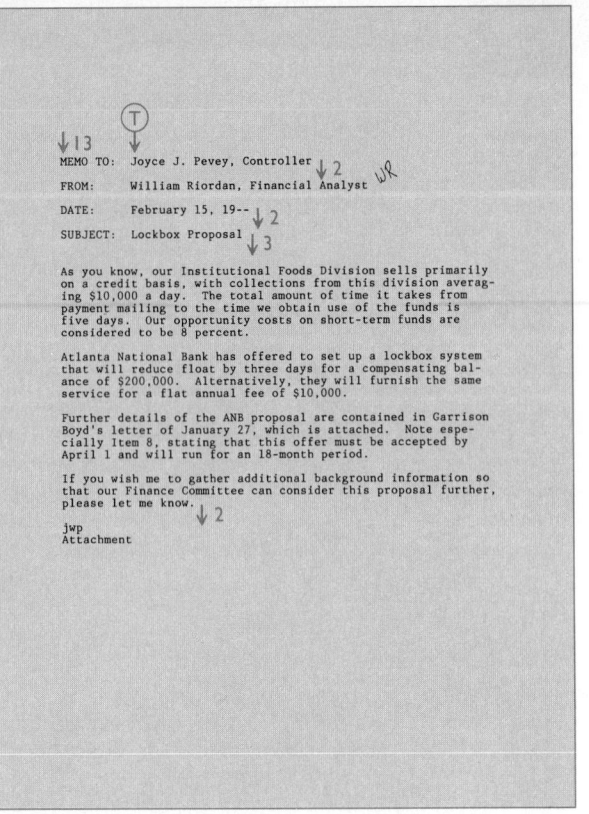

INTEROFFICE MEMORANDUM (Plain Paper)

STANDARD FORMAT FOR REPORTS

Line length: 6-inch (60 pica/70 elite)
Bound: Move both margins and all tab stops
　　　　　3 spaces to the right.
Paragraphs: indented 5 spaces
Spacing: double
Top margin: 2 inches (page 1);
　　　　　　1 inch (other pages)
Bottom margin: at least 1 inch

UNBOUND REPORT (Page 1)

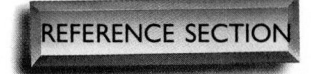

UNBOUND REPORT WITH FOOTNOTES (Page 2)

↓7
2
↓3

at the top right on line 7, with the first line of text beginning on the third line below the page number. The page number
is typed without the word Page. The page number of the first
page of a special section, such as the bibliography, is centered on line 7 from the bottom of the page.
↓3

MARGINS

The following margins should be used for a report:
↓2
1. A 6-inch line (60 pica spaces and 70 elite spaces). If
4→the report is to be bound at the left, move both margins
and all tab stops 3 spaces to the right.

2. A 2-inch top margin on the first page and a 1-inch top
margin on all other pages of the body of the report.

3. A 1-inch bottom margin on all pages.
↓3

REFERENCE CITATIONS

Reference citations supply the reader with specific references to sources used in preparing the report. According to
Turabian, "Short . . . quotations should be incorporated into
the text of the paper and enclosed in double quotation marks."[1]

For longer quotations, Daly stipulates:
↓2
5→A quotation that contains four or more typewritten ←5
lines should be set off from the text in single
spacing and indented 5 spaces from both margins,
with no quotation marks at the beginning or end.
Double-space before and after the quotation.[2] ↓1
↓2
_____
[1]Kate L. Turabian, A Manual for Writers of Term Papers,
Theses, and Dissertations, 4th ed., The University of Chicago
Press, Chicago, 1973, p. 64. ↓2

[2]Ferdinand J. Daly, "Formatting for Electronic Applications," Journal of Academic Research, Vol. 24, No. 3, September
1988, p. 49.

UNBOUND REPORT WITH FOOTNOTES (Partial Page)

↓7
3
↓3

Footnotes. Footnote citations are typed at the bottom
of the page on which the references occur and are separated
from the text by a line of underscores 2 inches long. Single-
space before and double-space after the divider line. Each
footnote is indented and single-spaced, with double spacing
used between footnotes. On a partial page, the divider line
and the footnotes go at the bottom of the page.[3]

Endnotes. Endnotes perform the same function as footnotes except that they are numbered consecutively throughout
the report and are typed on a separate NOTES page at the end
of the report.[4] The notes are single-spaced, with double
spacing between them. The identifying number is typed on the
line (not as a superior figure), followed by a period and 2
spaces.

_____
↓2
[3]William A. Sabin, The Gregg Reference Manual, 6th ed.,
McGraw-Hill, New York, 1985, p. 335.

[4]Ibid., p. 337.
↑7

BOUND REPORT WITH ENDNOTE REFERENCES

↓7
2
↓3

at the top right on line 7, with the first line of text beginning on the third line below the page number. The page number
is typed without the word Page. The page number of the first
page of a special section, such as the bibliography, is centered on line 7 from the bottom of the page.
↓3

MARGINS

The following margins should be used for a report:
↓2
1. A 6-inch line (60 pica spaces and 70 elite spaces). If
4→the report is to be bound at the left, move both margins
and all tab stops 3 spaces to the right.

2. A 2-inch top margin on the first page and a 1-inch top
margin on all other pages of the body of the report.

3. A 1-inch bottom margin on all pages.
↓3

REFERENCE CITATIONS ↓2

Reference citations supply the reader with specific references to sources used in preparing the report. According to
Turabian, "Short . . . quotations should be incorporated into
the text of the paper and enclosed in double quotation marks."[1]

For longer quotations, Daly stipulates:

5→A quotation that contains four or more typewritten ←5
lines should be set off from the text in single
spacing and indented 5 spaces from both margins,
with no quotation marks at the beginning or end.
Double-space before and after the quotation.[2] ↓2

Footnotes. Footnote citations are typed at the bottom
of the page on which the references occur and are separated
from the text by a line of underscores 2 inches long. Single-
space before and double-space after the divider line. Each

ENDNOTES FOR BOUND REPORT

↓13
NOTES
↓3

1. Kate L. Turabian, A Manual for Writers of Term
Papers, Theses, and Dissertations, 4th ed., The University
of Chicago Press, Chicago, 1973, p. 64. ↓2

2. Ferdinand J. Daly, "Formatting for Electronic Applications," Journal of Academic Research, Vol. 24, No. 3,
September 1988, p. 49.

3. William A. Sabin, The Gregg Reference Manual, 6th
ed., McGraw-Hill, New York, 1985, p. 335.

4. Ibid., p. 337.

5. Angela L. Boxer, A Manual of Style for Graduate
School, 3d ed., Consortium of Graduate Schools of Education,
Los Angeles, 1987, pp. 34-35.

6. Daly, p. 50.

7. H. L. Matthews, "New Research Reporting Standards,"
The New York Examiner, September 18, 1988, p. A2.

9
↑7

TITLE PAGE

↓13

TYPING FORMAL REPORTS

Formatting Guidelines for Typists

Line 33 → A Report Prepared for

ADS 301: Business Research

Professor Norman Pendergraft

Prepared by

Hiroshi Yoshimoto

November 18, 19--

↑13

TITLE PAGE

TABLE OF CONTENTS

Ⓜ ↓13

CONTENTS ↓3

TABLE OF CONTENTS

BIBLIOGRAPHY

↓13

BIBLIOGRAPHY ↓3

Boxer, Angela L., _A Manual of Style for Graduate School_,
5 → 3d ed., Consortium of Graduate Schools of Education,
   Los Angeles, 1987.

Daly, Ferdinand J., "Formatting for Electronic Applications,"
   Journal of Academic Research, Vol. 24, No. 3, September
   1988, pp. 46-50.

Matthews, H. L., "New Research Reporting Standards," _The New
   York Examiner_, September 18, 1988.

Sabin, William A., _The Gregg Reference Manual_, 6th ed.,
   McGraw-Hill, New York, 1985.

Salerno, Nicholas, et al., "How to Communicate With Your
   Typist," _Journal of Modern Communication_, Vol. 14, No.
   8, December 1988, pp. 25-27.

"You Can Type Your Research Report Yourself," _Current Business Careers_, June 19, 1987, pp. 39-42.

12

↑7

BIBLIOGRAPHY

OUTLINE

Ⓜ ↓13 TYPING FORMAL REPORTS ↓3

I.   HEADINGS ↓2

   A. Side Headings
   B. Paragraph Headings ↓3

II. MARGINS

   A. Top Margin
   B. Bottom Margin
   C. Side Margins
       1. Unbound Report
       2. Bound Report

III. REFERENCE CITATIONS

   A. Footnote References
   B. Endnotes
   C. Numbered Bibliography

IV. SUPPLEMENTARY PAGES

   A. Front Matter
       1. Title Page
       2. Table of Contents
   B. Appendix
   C. Bibliography

|←——Centered——→|

OUTLINE

MAJOR PARTS OF AN ELECTRONIC TYPEWRITER

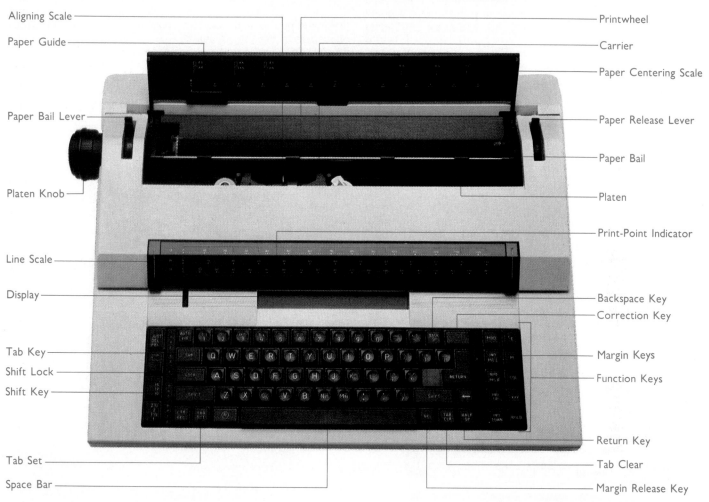

Aligning Scale
Paper Guide
Paper Bail Lever
Platen Knob
Line Scale
Display
Tab Key
Shift Lock
Shift Key
Tab Set
Space Bar

Printwheel
Carrier
Paper Centering Scale
Paper Release Lever
Paper Bail
Platen
Print-Point Indicator
Backspace Key
Correction Key
Margin Keys
Function Keys
Return Key
Tab Clear
Margin Release Key

ALIGNING SCALE. Aids in positioning the carrier on a line of text for inserting or deleting characters.

BACKSPACE KEY. Moves the carrier to the left 1 space at a time.

CARRIER. Moves from left to right, carrying the printwheel across the paper.

CORRECTION KEY. Engages correction tape and lifts off an error.

DISPLAY. Allows the typist to view the text as it is typed into memory and before it is printed on the paper.

FUNCTION KEYS. Perform special functions, such as auto-matic centering and moving to the beginning or end of the document.

LINE SCALE. Indicates horizontal spaces across the length of the platen, carrier position, and margin stops.

MARGIN KEYS. Used to set left and right margins.

MARGIN RELEASE KEY. Temporarily unlocks the left or right margin.

PAPER BAIL. Holds the paper against the platen.

PAPER-BAIL LEVER. Controls the paper bail.

PAPER CENTERING SCALE. Used to center any size of paper in the machine.

PAPER GUIDE. Guides and aligns the paper as it is inserted into the machine.

PAPER RELEASE LEVER. Loosens the paper for straightening or removing.

PLATEN. Large cylinder around which the paper is rolled.

PLATEN KNOB. Used to turn the platen by hand. The *variable platen* in the left platen knob can be pushed in to turn the platen freely for slight vertical adjustments.

PRINT-POINT INDICATOR. Shows the exact point on the line at which the next character will be printed.

PRINTWHEEL. A printing ele-ment that has each character engraved at the end of a spoke. When a key is struck, the print-wheel spins and prints the corre-sponding character.

RETURN KEY. Returns the car-rier to the start of a new line.

SHIFT KEY. Positions the car-rier so that a capital letter can be typed.

SHIFT LOCK. Locks the shift key so that the machine prints in all capitals.

SPACE BAR. Moves the carrier to the right 1 space at a time.

TAB CLEAR. Removes tabs.

TAB KEY. Moves the carrier to a point where a tab has been set.

TAB SET. Sets tabs at desired points.

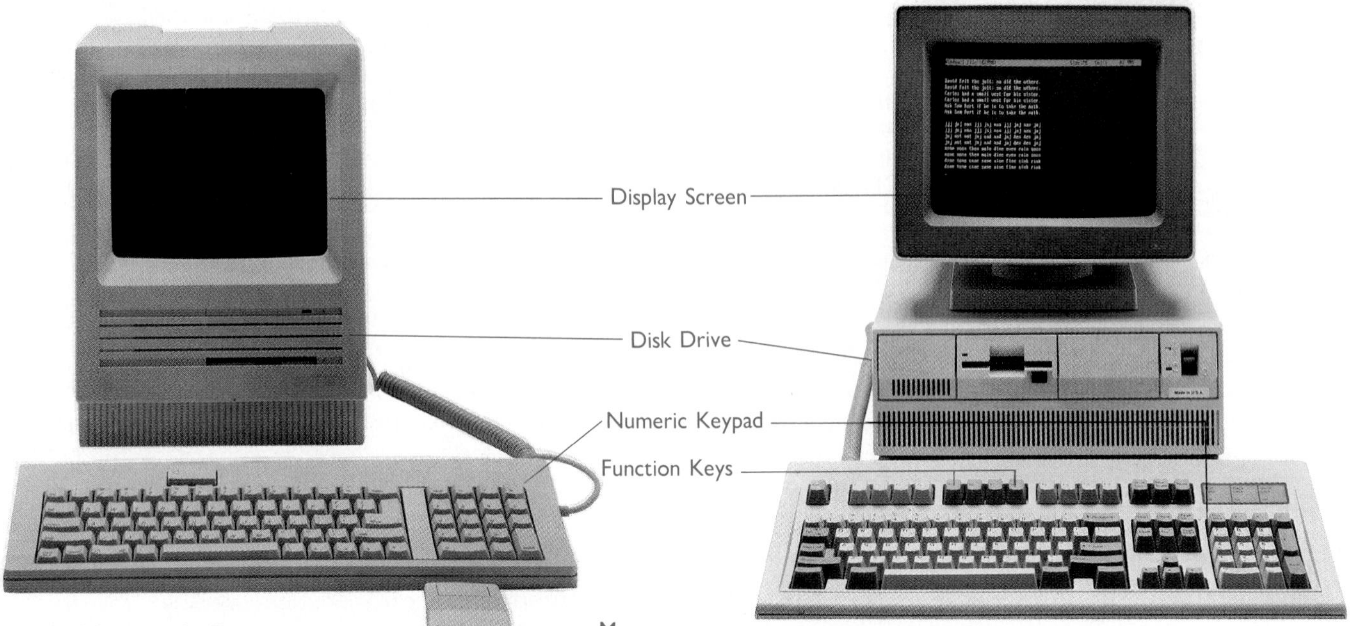

Display Screen

Disk Drive

Numeric Keypad

Function Keys

Apple Macintosh Computer

Mouse

IBM Personal Computer (PS/2)

Printer

DISK DRIVE. The component into which a diskette is inserted so that data can be read from or written onto the diskette.

DISPLAY SCREEN. A device similar to a television screen used to display text and graphics. Also called a monitor.

FUNCTION KEYS. Keys that perform special functions, such as saving a document, centering a line, or moving the cursor to the beginning or end of a document.

MOUSE. A hand-operated electronic device used to move the cursor around on the display screen.

NUMERIC KEYPAD. The ten number keys arranged in calculator style to allow one-handed touch-typing of numeric data.

PRINTER. The component that prints the copy on paper.

INTRODUCTION

BASIC MACHINE ADJUSTMENTS

COUNTING THE SPACES

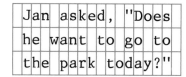

When a key or the space bar is tapped, the carrier advances 1 space. On most typewriters each space is the same size because most machines space uniformly, as though they were printing on graph paper.

These spaces can be counted by using the line scale. This scale shows a number every fifth or tenth space so that you can find any particular space across the width of the paper.

Each machine also has a special marker (called the carrier position indicator or the print-point indicator) that points to the space at which the machine is ready to print. For example, if the marker points to 58, the machine is ready to print at 58.

TYPE SIZE

```
1234567890      Pica
123456789012    Elite
```

Most typewriters use either *pica* or *elite* type. *Pica* type (also called 10 pitch) is larger than elite and prints 10 characters to an inch. *Elite* type (also called 12 pitch) prints 12 characters to an inch.

Thus a full line of typing on a standard sheet of paper (8½ inches wide) will contain 85 pica characters (8½ × 10) or 102 elite characters (8½ × 12).

Many electronic typewriters and computer printers also have other type sizes. For example, some machines print 15 characters to an inch, while others have proportional spacing, which means that small letters (such as *i*) require less space than large letters (such as *m* or *w*).

Although distinctions between pica and elite size type do not matter in forms, tables, or drills, these distinctions are important in letters and reports, because line lengths are commonly expressed in inches.

Find out which size type your machine has by typing the numbers 1 through 0 and comparing your typed copy with the illustration above.

PLANNING MARGINS AND SETTING MARGIN STOPS

Margin stops are used to center typed material across the paper. To plan the left and right margin settings:

Left Margin.   Subtract half the desired line length from the center point. For example, for a 60-space line, subtract 30 from the centering point you are using.

Right Margin.   Add half the desired line length to the center point plus 5 extra spaces to allow for line-ending decisions. See the table below.

MARGIN SETTINGS

Type Size	Line Length Spaces	Line Length Inches	Margin Settings Left	Margin Settings Right
Pica	40	4″	22	67
	50	5″	17	72
	60	6″	12	77
	70	7″	7	82
Elite	40	3⅓″	30	75
	50*	4″	25	80
	60	5″	20	85
	70*	6″	15	90

*Rounded off.

Margin Stops.   Margin stops for electronic typewriters are typically set by moving the carrier to the correct point on the margin scale and then depressing either the left or the right margin key.

Margin stops for electric typewriters can be set by pushing in the left and right margin stops and sliding them to the correct settings on the line scale.

On a computer, the word processing software generally has a default (preset) margin setting. To change the margin settings, consult the operating instructions provided by the manufacturer or ask your instructor for assistance.

SETTING TABS

Tab settings enable you to indent paragraphs consistently and to format columns of data efficiently. To set tabs:

1. Clear all tabs already set. On electronic typewriters, depress the tab clear key wherever a tab has been set. On electric typewriters, move the carrier to the right margin, and then hold down the tab clear key as you return the carrier. Software commands control the tab settings in word processing.
2. Set a new tab. Depress the space bar the number of spaces you wish to indent (usually 5 for a paragraph indention), and press the tab set key.
3. Test the new tab setting. Return the carrier to the left margin, and then firmly depress the tab key. The carrier should move directly to the point where you set the tab.
Note: You will not have to set any tabs until Lesson 10.

SETTING LINE SPACING

The amount of space between lines of typing is controlled by a line space selector (electric typewriters), by a line space key (electronic typewriters), or by a software command (word processing software).

On a typewriter, set the controls at 1 for single spacing (no blank space between lines) and at 2 for double spacing (1 blank line between typed lines). Some machines also have 1½ spacing (½ blank line between typed lines) and triple spacing (2 blank lines between typed lines).

LINE SPACING

Set at 1	Set at 1½	Set at 2	Set at 3
single	one and a half	double	triple
single			
single	one and a half	double	
single	one and a half		triple

INSERTING PAPER

To insert paper into the machine:

1. Confirm the paper guide setting.
2. Pull the paper bail forward.
3. With your left hand, place the paper behind the platen and against the paper guide. Use your right hand to turn the right platen knob clockwise to draw in the paper. Advance the paper until about a third of the sheet is visible.

Note: Electronic typewriters automatically feed the paper into the machine.

4. Check that the paper is straight by aligning the left edges of the front and back against the paper guide.

If the edges of the paper do not align, pull the paper release lever forward, straighten the paper, and then push the paper release lever back.

5. Place the paper bail back against the paper. Adjust the small rollers on the paper bail so that they are spaced evenly across the paper.

6. To prepare to type, turn the paper back until about ¼ inch shows above the paper bail.

REMOVING PAPER

To remove paper from the machine:

1. Pull the paper bail forward.
2. Pull the paper release lever toward you with your right hand as you silently draw out the paper with your left hand.
3. Return the paper release lever and paper bail to their normal positions.

DAILY ROUTINE

Perform these steps at the start of each class:

1. Arrange your work area: typewriter even with the front edge of the desk; typing paper on one side of the machine and textbook on the other, tilted for ease of reading.
2. Open the textbook to the correct lesson, and note the directions in the heading.
3. Make the necessary machine adjustments—set margins, tabs, and line spacing.
4. Insert a sheet of paper; straighten it if necessary.
5. Assume the correct typing posture, and (starting with Lesson 2) begin typing the Warmup drill for the lesson.

TYPING POSTURE

Typing speed and accuracy are both affected by your posture.

Body centered opposite the J key, leaning forward.

Head erect, turned to face the book.

Feet apart and firmly braced.

Wrists straight and fingers curved. Position your fingertips on the home keys: left hand on A, S, D, and F; right hand on J, K, L, and ; (semicolon).

Note: Do not rest your hands or wrists on the equipment or on the desk.

WORD PROCESSING

The symbol above is designed to call your attention to information about word processing concepts or applications that you will encounter throughout this text. These special notations are provided to help you understand how word processing equipment functions if used in place of a typewriter to format documents.

Although you may not have access to word processing equipment at this time, you should be familiar with its capabilities: you can be sure that you will have occasion to use it—either in school or on the job—in the very near future.

COMPUTER SOFTWARE

The miniature disk pictured above appears throughout the book as a reminder to use the correlated software—if you are learning to type on a computer rather than a typewriter.

BUILDING AND MEASURING SKILL

To develop speed when typing drill lines, repeat each *individual* line the designated number of times. To emphasize accuracy, repeat each *group* of lines (as though it were a paragraph) the designated number of times.

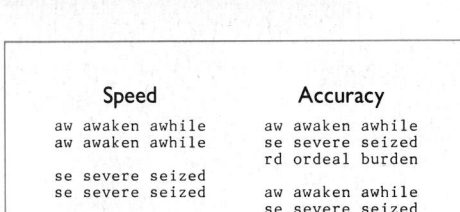

Speed	Accuracy
aw awaken awhile	aw awaken awhile
aw awaken awhile	se severe seized
	rd ordeal burden
se severe seized	
se severe seized	aw awaken awhile
	se severe seized
rd ordeal burden	rd ordeal burden
rd ordeal burden	

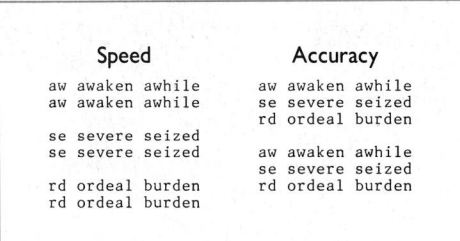

```
        Stop just a moment s
    4                        5
typing position.  Your ba
                    8
and your body should lean
              11
wrists should be low, wit
    14                  15
that you can strike the k
```

All timed writings in this text are the exact length needed to reach the speed goal for the lesson. Thus, if you finish the timed writing, you know you have reached your speed goal.

Beginning with the 3-minute timing in Lesson 22, all timed writings contain small numbers, called speed markers, above the copy. Your word-a-minute (wam) typing speed is the last number that you reach.

PART I

THE TYPEWRIT
THE ALPHABET
AND NUMBER KEYS

OBJECTIVES

KEYBOARDING SKILL

To operate the letter and number keys by touch.

To make all machine adjustments needed to set margins, tabs, and line spacing; to remove paper efficiently.

To type 28 words a minute on a 2-minute timed writing with no more than 5 errors.

PROOFREADING SKILL

To proofread typewritten copy, mark and count errors, and compute typing speed.

TECHNICAL SKILL

To answer correctly at least 90 percent of the questions on an objective test.

FORMATTING SKILL

To center typed material both horizontally and vertically.

■ To understand how word processing hardware and software would function if used to format various production assignments.

SALE OF PHOENIX PHANTOMS

By Eileen Turner

On November 19, 1987, the Consolidated Football league (CLF) approved the sale of the Phoenix Phantoms for #23 million dollars to a group of ten investors known as Sports Invest, Inc.[1] This sale officially ended the 20-year ownership of the team by Mrs. L. #J. Boggs of Tempe, Arizona, and New York City.

OPERATIONAL MANAGEMENT

Louis Olivas was named managing partner of the new partnership and was given the voting trust, which gives him the power to represent the Phantoms in CFL matters. This action eliminates any real need for a single majority owner.

Still, as Olivas has himself pointed out, "The owners can always exercise their right to replace me if they wish."[23]

FORM OF NEW OWNERSHIP

The new owners are a group of 10 Arizona business people who have formed a Limited Partnership. They range in age from 33 to 65 and in ownership from 3% to 17%.[32]

---

[1]Ron Turner, "Phantoms Have New Owner--Finally," The Arizona Herald, September 15, 1987, p. C-2.

[32]Andrew Shafley, "Does Phoenix have a Phantom Boss?" Sports Monthly, October, 1987, p. 114.

[23]Ibid.

SS

Please prepare Purchase Order 186, current date, to Software Plus, 2505 Main Street, Stratford, CT 06497.

Qty	Description	Stock No.	Price	Total
1	Ticketmaster software program version 3.2	807X	298.00	298.00
5	Time / Date utility	243T	39.95	199.75
2	Universal spelling checker	349S	89.95	179.90
	Total			677.65
	Shipping			78.50
	Total Amount Due			756.15

Line: 40 spaces
Spacing: single
Drills: 2 times
Workguide: 9–12
Format Guide: 3–4
Tape: IA or KIA
K = Keyboard
      Presentation
      Tapes

HOME KEYS

SPACE BAR

Goal: To control the home keys (A S D F J K L ;) and space bar.

I-A. PRACTICE THE SPACE BAR

With all fingers held motionless in home position, poise your right thumb about ¼ inch above the space bar. Tap the space bar in its center, and bounce your thumb off.

Space once (*tap the space bar once*) . . . twice (*tap the space bar twice*) . . . once . . . once . . . twice . . . once . . . twice . . . once . . . twice . . . twice . . . once . . . once . . . Repeat.

I-B. PRACTICE THE RETURN/ENTER KEY

On many computers, the return key is called *the enter key.*

In a quick, stabbing motion (1) extend the fourth finger of your right hand to the return key; (2) lightly tap the return key, causing the carrier to return automatically; and (3) "zip" the finger back to its home-key position.

Practice using the return key until you can do so with confidence and without raising your eyes from the book.

Space once . . . twice . . . once . . . twice . . . Return! Home! (*fingers on home keys*) . . . Repeat.

I-C. PRACTICE THE FOREFINGER KEYS

I-C. Using your right thumb and both forefingers (with other fingers in home position), type these three lines. Tap the keys lightly. Do not space after the last letter in the line before the return.

Left forefinger on F key
Right thumb on space bar

fff fff ff ff f f ff ff f f

Right forefinger on J key
Right thumb on space bar

jjj jjj jj jj j j jj jj j j

Left forefinger on F key
Right forefinger on J key
Right thumb on space bar

fff jjj ff jj f j ff jj f j

Ask your instructor for the General Information Test on Part 3.

T E S T 3

PROGRESS TEST ON PART 3

TEST 3-A
3-MINUTE TIMED WRITING

Line: 60 spaces
Tab: 5
Paper: Workguide 113

```
       1          2            3              4
A limited partnership is a form of business enterprise    12
     5          6           7              8
in which all the risks of one or more of the owners will be   24
         9           10            11           12
restricted to the amount of assets each has invested in the   36
        13          14          15           16
firm.  This type of firm should have at least one owner who   48
         17          18           19          20
would assume the debts of the firm when called on to do so.   60
       21          22           23          24
Since limited partners will minimize their losses, they may   72
         25           26          27          28
not take part in running the new firm.  Because the expense   84
         29           30          31           32
of running some businesses is growing so quickly, this form   96
        33          34          35           36
of stock ownership has enjoyed much acceptance, most of all   108
       37          38          39           40
in high-risk industries such as in sports or entertainment.   120
 |  |  | 2 | 3 | 4 | 5 | 6 | 7 | 8 | 9 | 10 | 11 | 12
```

TEST 3-B
LETTER 22
MODIFIED-BLOCK STYLE

Paper: Workguide 115

Use the current date.

Treat each item in the enumeration as a separate paragraph.

Please send the following letter to Mr. R. J. Caldwell, General Counsel / Consolidated Football League / 1603 Evans Street / Reston, VA 22091 / Dear Mr. Caldwell:

This letter will serve as official notification that ten investors have   41
completed their purchase of the Phoenix Phantoms from Mrs. L. J. Boggs.   56
The names, addresses, amount of investment, and affiliations of these ten   71
investors are given in the enclosed listing.   79

Mr. Thomas Keller will assume the role of general partner. The other   93
nine partners will be limited partners. Their rights will be restricted in   109
the following manner: 113

1. Their names will not appear in the name of the business.   125

2. They will be silent partners and will not be allowed to participate   139
in management.   142

3. They will not provide any services for the firm. This restriction   156
includes business as well as professional services.   166

The new management team will be in place on July 1. We look forward   180
to continuing the excellent working relationship established between   194
the former owner and the CFL.   200

Sincerely, / Patricia Muranka / Administrative Manager / *(Your initials)* / Enclosure   209
    212

LEFT HAND
Forefinger   F
Second finger   D
Third finger   S
Fourth finger   A

RIGHT HAND
J   Forefinger
K   Second finger
L   Third finger
;   Fourth finger
Space bar   Thumb

SPACE BAR

Leave 1 blank line (return twice) before starting a new drill.

1-D. PRACTICE THE F AND J KEYS

Use the forefingers on F and J keys. Tap the space bar with your right thumb.

1 fff fff jjj jjj fff jjj ff jj ff jj f j
   fff fff jjj jjj fff jjj ff jj ff jj f j

1-E. PRACTICE THE D AND K KEYS

Use the second fingers.

2 ddd ddd kkk kkk ddd kkk dd kk dd kk d k
   ddd ddd kkk kkk ddd kkk dd kk dd kk d k

1-F. PRACTICE THE S AND L KEYS

Use the third fingers.

3 sss sss lll lll sss lll ss ll ss ll s l
   sss sss lll lll sss lll ss ll ss ll s l

1-G. PRACTICE THE A AND ; KEYS

Use the fourth fingers.

4 aaa aaa ;;; ;;; aaa ;;; aa ;; aa ;; a ;
   aaa aaa ;;; ;;; aaa ;;; aa ;; aa ;; a ;

1-H. WORD BUILDING: SHORT WORDS

Type lines 5–11 two times each. Leave a blank line after each pair. Note word patterns.

5 lll aaa ddd lad lad fff aaa ddd fad fad

6 ddd aaa ddd dad dad aaa sss kkk ask ask

7 aaa sss ;;; as; as; aaa ddd ;;; ad; ad;

1-I. WORD BUILDING: LONGER WORDS

Space once after a semicolon.

8 a ad add adds; l la lad lads; a ad ads;

9 f fa fad fads; a as ask asks; d da dad;

10 l la las lass; f fa fal fall; s sa sad;

Compare your Lesson 1 typing with that shown on Workguide pages 9–10, and then complete Workguide pages 11 and 12.

1-J. SKILL MEASUREMENT

11 a dad; a fall; ask a lass; add a salad;

60-F. FORMS REVIEW

MEMO 10
Paper: Workguide 109

Send a memo dated December 2, 19— to the Personnel Department and Credit Union from Lisa Chiaverotti, Records Administrator, on the subject of Credit Verification.

I have recently applied for an automobile loan in the amount of $7,800 from City Imports in Fort Worth. As part of the loan process, I was required to complete the attached application for credit. I feel sure that City Imports will be contacting you to verify my employment and the amount in my credit-union account.   36 50 65 79 86

You will note that I gave my salary level as of this coming January 1. Since that will be my salary during the period of the loan, I felt that it was appropriate to do so. Also, please note that although I had a credit-union loan for $500, that loan was repaid in full on November 1.   100 116 131 143

I would appreciate your furnishing any information requested by City Imports. Please let me know if you have any questions.   157 168

(Your initials) / Attachment   170

FORM 6
APPLICATION FOR CREDIT
Paper: Workguide 111

APPLICATION FOR CREDIT

NAME _Lisa Chiaverotti_

ADDRESS _1801 North Lake Drive_

Fort Worth ___ _TX_ ___ _76135_
Town or City ____ State ____ ZIP

HOW LONG AT ABOVE ADDRESS? _2½ years_

OWN OR RENT? _Own_

PREVIOUS ADDRESS _118 Harris Street, Apt. 3-B_

Fort Worth ___ _TX_ ___ _76104_
Town or City ____ State ____ ZIP

CURRENT EMPLOYER _Worldwide Airlines_

EMPLOYER'S ADDRESS _2000 Cleveland Street_

Dallas ___ _TX_ ___ _75215_
Town or City ____ State ____ ZIP

POSITION HELD _Records Administrator_

HOW LONG EMPLOYED? _6 years_

CURRENT SALARY _$27,600 a year_

SOCIAL SECURITY NUMBER _187-92-4036_

TELEPHONE _(817) 555-3180_

CHECKING ACCOUNT _City National Bank_
____ Name of Bank

SAVINGS ACCOUNT _Worldwide Credit Union_
____ Name of Bank

OTHER CREDIT OBLIGATIONS

Federal Mortgage Corp. ___ _$68,000_
Creditor ____ Amount

City Card ___ _$475_
Creditor ____ Amount

NAMES AND ADDRESSES OF TWO REFERENCES

Christopher Cardin, Manager, City National Bank
P.O. Box 1076, Dallas, TX 75221
Harriet Wolf, Publisher, Worldwide Airlines
2000 Cleveland St., Dallas, TX 75215

APPLICANT'S SIGNATURE _____

Line: 40 spaces
Spacing: single
Drills: 2 times
Format Guide: 3–4
Tape: 2A or K2A

Goal: To control the H, E, O, and R keys.

From now on, your fingers are named for the home keys on which they rest. For example, the D finger is the second finger on the left hand.

Use the J finger.

Note: Leave 1 space after a semicolon.

Use the D finger.

Use the L finger.

Use the F finger.

2-A. WARMUP

1 fff jjj ddd kkk sss lll aaa ;;; fff jjj
2 ask a lass; a fad; alas a lad; a salad;

2-B. PRACTICE THE **H** KEY

3 jjj jhj jhj hjh jjj jhj jhj hjh jjj jhj
4 has has had had aha aha ash ash hah hah
5 shah shad hall dash lash sash half hash
6 add a dash; a lass has half; as dad had

2-C. PRACTICE THE **E** KEY

7 ddd ded ded ede ddd ded ded ede ddd ded
8 led fee lee sea fed ade she he; see lea
9 feed held lead ease seal head fake keel
10 she sees a shed; he led a lass; a lease

2-D. PRACTICE THE **O** KEY

11 lll lol lol olo lll lol lol olo lll lol
12 sod old ode odd oak oh; hod foe off doe
13 oleo solo does odes joke kook look shoe
14 she held a lease; a lad solos; old oak;

2-E. PRACTICE THE **R** KEY

15 fff frf frf rfr fff frf frf rfr fff frf
16 red are her oar rod era rah err ore ark
17 door rare role read fare dear soar oars
18 she offered a rare jar; a dark red oar;

Line: 60 spaces
Tab: 5
Spacing: single
Drills: 2 times
Workguide: 107–111
Format Guide: 51–52
Tape: 25B

LESSON
60

SKILLBUILDING AND FORMS REVIEW

Goals: To type 40 wam/3'/5e; to review forms typing.

60-A. WARMUP

S 1 A bushel of corn was thrown to the turkeys by the neighbor.
A 2 Did Weldon give Liz your picturesque jukebox for Christmas?
3 3 Read pages 467–518 carefully for the weekend of July 29–30.

SKILLBUILDING

60-B. PROGRESSIVE PRACTICE: ALPHABET

Turn to the Progressive Practice: Alphabet routine at the back of the book. Take several 30-second timings, starting at the speed at which you left off the last time. Record your progress on Workguide page 5.

60-C. All of these words are among the 125 most misspelled words in business correspondence.

60-C. PRODUCTION PRACTICE: SPELLING

4 their system through services received personnel appreciate
5 which during further interest material committee commission
6 there office general required schedule employees management
7 prior please present benefits business necessary procedures
8 first policy account provided contract available production

60-D. Tab: Every 11 spaces.

60-D. TECHNIQUE TYPING: TAB KEY

9 alas   away   aqua   area   aura   able
10 abut   aces   acid   acre   acts   arch
11 adds   aide   aged   awed   anew   apes
12 ache   ante   airy   ally   also   amid

60-E. Spacing: double. Record your score.

60-E. SKILL MEASUREMENT: 3-MINUTE TIMED WRITING

13   High-level spelling skills are the true mark of expert   12
14 typists. If your own skills are quite weak, begin today to   24
15 try to improve them. To begin with, learn how to spell all   36
16 the words in the above list. Next, start keeping a journal   48
17 of all words that you type that give you spelling problems.   60
18 After you have a page or two of such words, analyze them to   72
19 see if there is a pattern to your misspellings. Do most of   84
20 your words involve word beginnings or endings? Do many in-   96
21 volve similar-sounding words? Your journal can help you to   108
22 identify any problems to make your studying more efficient.   120
   | 1 | 2 | 3 | 4 | 5 | 6 | 7 | 8 | 9 | 10 | 11 | 12

2-F. BUILD SKILL ON WORD FAMILIES

Do not pause at the vertical lines that mark off the word families.

19 sold fold hold old; | hale sale kale dale
20 sash dash lash ash; | seed heed deed feed
21 rear sear dear ear; | rake sake fake lake

2-G. Take three 1-minute timings. Try to complete both lines each time.

2-G. SKILL MEASUREMENT: 1-MINUTE TIMED WRITING

22 she heard dad ask for a roll; she asked
23 for a jar;

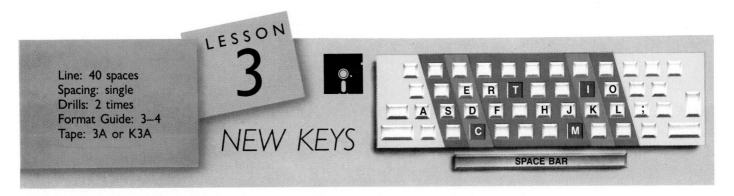

LESSON

3

NEW KEYS

Line: 40 spaces
Spacing: single
Drills: 2 times
Format Guide: 3–4
Tape: 3A or K3A

SPACE BAR

Goal: To control the M, T, I, and C keys.

3-A. WARMUP

1 aa ;; ss ll dd kk ff jj hh ee oo rr aa;
2 he fed a doe; she sold a dark red shoe;

3-B. PRACTICE THE M KEY

Use the J finger.

3 jjj jmj jmj mjm jjj jmj jmj mjm jjj jmj
4 mar ham ma; ram dam me; jam am; mom mad
5 same lame room fame make roam loam arms
6 she made more room for more of her jam;

3-C. PRACTICE THE T KEY

Use the F finger.

7 fff ftf ftf tft fff ftf ftf tft fff ftf
8 tar ate sat lot mat tam rat eat jot hot
9 tool fate mart date late told take mate
10 she took the tools from store to store;

TABLE 13

Spacing: single
Paper: full sheet

WORLDWIDE AIRLINES MONTHLY SUMMARY		7
Description	_Balance_	10
Previous balance	28,500	15
Credit miles added	5,000	19
Credit miles used for award	20,000	26
Current balance	13,500	30
Miles to next award	6,500	35

TABLE 14

Spacing: single
Paper: full sheet

WORLDWIDE FREQUENT-FLIER AWARDS   6

(Awards Issued Automatically)   12

Mileage	Airline Awards	Car-Rental Awards	
			20
10,000	1 first-class upgrade	1 large-car upgrade	29
20,000	1 domestic ticket	1 weekend day rental	37
30,000	1 international ticket	2 weekend day rentals	47
40,000	2 domestic tickets	2 weekday rentals	55
50,000	2 international tickets	3 weekday rentals	65

TABLE 15

Spacing: single
Paper: full sheet

WORLDWIDE AIRLINES MILEAGE STATEMENT   7

July 19—   9

Date	Flight Number	Itinerary	Credit Miles	
				11
				16
07/10/—	2806	Lansing, MI–Detroit, MI	500	24
07/10/—	143	Detroit, MI–Philadelphia, PA	1,000	33
07/14/—	235	Philadelphia, PA–Detroit, MI	1,000	41
07/14/—	2757	Detroit, MI–Lansing, MI	500	49
07/23/—	186	Detroit, MI–Boston, MA	1,000	57
07/24/—	456	Boston, MA–Detroit, MI	1,000	64

3-D.   PRACTICE THE **I** KEY

Use the K finger.

11 kkk kik kik iki kkk kik kik iki kkk kik
12 air lid did sit kit rim him sir dim fir
13 iris tide site item fire idea tile tire
14 this time he left his tie at the store;

3-E.   PRACTICE THE **C** KEY

Use the D finger.

15 ddd dcd dcd cdc ddd dcd dcd cdc ddd dcd
16 cot ace ice arc cat coo car act cod sac
17 deck coat itch aces face chat tack rich
18 he lets his old cat catch lots of mice;

3-F.   BUILD SKILL ON WORD FAMILIES

19 mace face lace ace; | sail tail rail fail
20 mire tire fire ire; | dots tots jots lots
21 jade fade made ade; | seed deed feed heed
22 fads cads lads ads; | hale tale sale dale

3-G.   BUILD SKILL ON SHORT SENTENCES

23 he told his joke; she is tired of them;
24 she took the feed seed to the old farm;
25 her date is late; she said he is ideal;
26 she met him at the dock; he liked that;

3-H. Take three 1-minute timings. Try to complete both lines each time.

3-H.   SKILL MEASUREMENT: 1-MINUTE TIMED WRITING

27 the local store had a fire sale to sell
28 off some old clocks;

Line: 60 spaces
Tab: 5, center
Spacing: single
Drills: 2 times
Format Guide: 49–51
Tape: 24B

LESSON 59

SKILLBUILDING AND TABLE REVIEW

Goals: To build speed and accuracy; to review table typing.

59-A. WARMUP

S 1 Mr. Leo Burns is such a busy man he may not go to the game.
A 2 Felix might hit your jackpot even with the bad quiz answer.
N 3 Read pages 486-537 in Chapter 19 of your text for March 20.

SKILLBUILDING

59-B. DIAGNOSTIC TYPING: NUMBERS

Turn to the Diagnostic Typing: Numbers routine at the back of the book. Take the Pretest, and record your performance on Workguide page 5. Then practice the drill lines for those reaches on which you made errors.

PRETEST. Take a 1-minute timing; compute your speed and count errors.

59-C. PRETEST: ALTERNATE- AND ONE-HAND WORDS

4   I will defer the amendment that will attract a minimum   12
5 of a million visitors eastward to the island since it might   24
6 have created a problem. Did the auditors turn down my bid?   36
  | 1 | 2 | 3 | 4 | 5 | 6 | 7 | 8 | 9 | 10 | 11 | 12

PRACTICE.
  Speed Emphasis: If you made 2 or fewer errors on the Pretest, type each line twice.
  Accuracy Emphasis: If you made 3 or more errors, type each group of lines (as though it were a paragraph) twice.

59-D. PRACTICE: ALTERNATE HANDS

7 visible signs amendment visual height turndown suspend maps
8 element amend endowment signal handle ornament auditor half
9 figment usual authentic emblem island clemency dormant snap
10 problem chair shamrocks profit thrown blandish penalty form

59-E. PRACTICE: ONE HAND

11 trade poplin greater pumpkin eastward plumply barrage holly
12 exact kimono created minikin cassette opinion seaweed union
13 defer unhook reserve minimum attracts million scatter plump
14 serve uphill exceeds killjoy carefree homonym terrace onion

POSTTEST. Repeat the Pretest and compare performance.

59-F. POSTTEST: ALTERNATE- AND ONE-HAND WORDS

59-G. Compare this footnote listing with that on page 119. Type a list of the words that contain errors, correcting the errors as you type.

59-G. PRODUCTION PRACTICE: PROOFREADING

15   [1]J. A. Lindrup, Cost-Effective Telecommunication
16 Management, The Business Press, New York, 1987, p. 284.
17   [2]Carolyn Thering, "How to Read a Telephone Bill, Telecom-
18 munication Quarterly, December, 1986, p. 386.
19   [3]Donald Macleod and Denis Lebsack, "Solving the Billing
20 Billing Maize," Monthly Business Review, May 1978, p. 113.
21   [4]Thering, op. cit., page 215.

Line: 40 spaces
Spacing: single
Drills: 2 times
Workguide: 13
Format Guide: 3–4
Tape: 4A or K4A

Goals: To control the right shift, V, and period keys; to count errors.

4-A. WARMUP

1 the jets had left as she came too late;
2 the farmer hired him to feed the mares;

To capitalize any letter that is on the left half of the keyboard:
1. With the J finger home, press and hold down the right shift key with the Sem finger.
2. Strike the letter key.
3. Release the shift key, and return fingers to home position.

4-B. PRACTICE THE RIGHT SHIFT KEY

3 ;;; ;A; ;A; ;;; ;S; ;S; ;;; ;D; ;D; ;;;
4 Ada Sam Rae Ted Dee Sam Tom Sal Alf Art
5 Dick Sara Todd Amos Carl Elsa Edie Chet
6 Amos Dale Ford married Emma Dee Carter;

4-C. PRACTICE THE V KEY

Use the F finger.

7 fff fvf fvf vfv fff fvf fvf vfv fff fvf
8 vie Ava vet Viv vis vim via Eva eve Val
9 vote move Vera vast ever Vida have live
10 Victor Vida moved to Vassar to see Eve;

4-D. PRACTICE THE · KEY

Use the L finger.

Space once after a period following an abbreviation but none after a period within an abbreviation. Space twice after a period at the end of a sentence.

11 111 1.1 1.1 .1. 111 1.1 1.1 .1. 111 1.1
12 sr. sr. dr. dr. ea. ea. Dr. Dr. Sr. Sr.
13 a.m. i.e. loc. cit. A.D. jr. D.C. misc.
14 She left. Sam cried. Sarah came home.

4-E. BUILD SKILL ON SHORT SENTENCES

Maintain a smooth and steady pace. Speed up on the second copy of each sentence.

15 Dr. Drake called Sam; he asked for Ted.
16 Vera told a tale to her old classmates.
17 Todd asked Cal to stack five old rails.
18 Del asked if he had read the last tale.

58-E. REPORT REVIEW

REPORT 19
TWO-PAGE UNBOUND REPORT WITH FOOTNOTES

Visual guide: Workguide 59

Decide where to end your page. See the note on page 99 for page-ending decisions.

HOW TO READ A TELEPHONE BILL 6

By Elaine Daniels 9

Only two out of ten corporations even bother to check their tele- 22
phone bills. Most pay them automatically, even though the average 35
corporate monthly bill is $94,000 and even though it's not impossible to 50
find that 25 percent of a bill has been overcharged.[1] 60

DECIPHERING THE BILL 64

Most managers find it difficult to pinpoint errors and decipher mul- 78
tipage telephone bills. To clarify charges on the portion of the bill 92
dealing with basic services, experts suggest calling the local telephone 107
company and requesting an itemization of all costs associated with 120
monthly service. 123

"The first thing a prudent manager should do is identify the various 137
codes and services to make sure the company is getting all the services 151
for which it is being charged," states Carolyn Thering, president of Ther- 166
ing Communication Services.[2] Frequently corporations find that they 180
are being billed for services that they thought had been disconnected. 194

Each footnote must go on the same page on which it is cited in the text.

Another communication consultant believes that the most frequent 207
errors are for services and equipment that at some point were discon- 220
nected; yet the charges remain on the monthly telephone bills.[3] The 234
only way to get such charges deleted from the phone company's billing 248
computer is to make a request in writing. 256

NEED FOR EXPERTS 260

A consultant may be able to pinpoint charges that can be eliminated 273
from a company's bill. Because of the complexity of telephone codes, 287
tariffs, and billing procedures, it is difficult for many office managers to 303
decipher bills effectively. 308

Most experts say that it is cost-effective to pay a trained consultant to 323
come in at least once every two years to analyze telephone equipment, 337
usage, and billing. It is not unusual to find that the consultant will end up 353
saving the company three to four times his or her fee in yearly billings 367
for telephone usage.[4] 371

____________ 375

[1]J. A. Lindrup, Cost-Effective Telecommunications Management, 388
The Business Press, New York, 1987, p. 284. 396

[2]Carolyn Thering, "How to Read a Phone Bill," Telecommunications 409
Quarterly, December 1986, p. 386. 416

[3]Donald MacLeod and Dennis Lebsack, "Solving the Billing Maze," 429
Monthly Business Review, May 1987, p. 113. 437

[4]Thering, op. cit., p. 215. 443

See the note on page 98 regarding the placement of footnotes on a partial page.

4-F. COUNTING ERRORS

Compare with lines 19–21 below.

(Davod) ordered steaks; Sal liked steaks,
David ordered steaks; Sal (likedsteaks).
Viola sold (m st) of the (items) at a loss.
Viola sold most the items at (at) a loss.
Al (him asked) for three jars of red jam.
Al asked him for three jars of red (jaj .

After studying 4-F, complete Workguide page 13.

As indicated in the examples above, count it an error when:

1. Any stroke is incorrect.
2. Any punctuation after a word is incorrect or omitted.
3. The spacing after a word or after its punctuation is incorrect.
4. Any stroke is so light that it does not show clearly.
5. One stroke is made over another.
6. A word is omitted.
7. A word is repeated.
8. Words are transposed.
9. A direction about spacing, indenting, and so on, is violated.
10. Only one error is charged to any one word, no matter how many errors it may contain.

4-G. After typing each line 2 times, circle and count your errors.

4-G. BUILD SKILL ON SHORT SENTENCES

19 David ordered steaks; Sal liked steaks.
20 Viola sold most of the items at a loss.
21 Al asked him for three jars of red jam.

4-H. Take three 1-minute timings. Try to complete both lines each time.

4-H. SKILL MEASUREMENT: 1-MINUTE TIMED WRITING

22 Ed asked them to tell the major to come
23 after Vic left for home.

LESSON 5

Line: 40 spaces
Spacing: single
Drills: 2 times
Workguide: 14
Format Guide: 3–4
Tape: 5A or K5A

REVIEW

Goals: To strengthen all controls; to learn how to measure speed.

5-A. WARMUP

1 The jet took Ed to Asia after the race.
2 Vera liked the meal; Art loved the jam.

SKILLBUILDING AND REPORT REVIEW

Line: 60 spaces
Tab: 5, center
Spacing: single
Drills: 2 times
Format Guide: 49–50
Tape: 25A

Goals: To type 40 wam/3'/5e; to review report typing.

58-A. WARMUP

S 1 The maid will make up some snacks for the ten men at eight.
A 2 Jack's conquests near Oxbow proved not to faze Gil's enemy.
N 3 Use a 70-space elite line for Reports 19-23 on pages 48-56.

SKILLBUILDING

58-B. Take a 1-minute timing on the first paragraph to establish your base speed. Then take several 1-minute timings on the remaining paragraphs. As soon as you equal or exceed your base speed on one paragraph, advance to the next one.

58-B. SUSTAINED TYPING: ROUGH DRAFT

4   The early typing courses taught students to type using   12
5 only the two forefingers. Each student decided for himself   24
6 which finger to use for each key; there was no consistency.   36
7   As a joke, someone once bragged to the reigning typing   12
8 champion that he could type with (8) fingers. The cham-   24
9 pion went home and taught himself to type that way.   36
10   It wasn't until after the second worldwar that typping   12
11 really caught on: the Government had increased need for   24
12 typists, so they taut the military to type by touch.   36

I I I 2 I 3 I 4 I 5 I 6 I 7 I 8 I 9 I 10 I 11 I 12

58-C. PROGRESSIVE PRACTICE: ALPHABET

Turn to the Progressive Practice: Alphabet routine at the back of the book. Take several 30-second timings, starting at the speed at which you left off the last time. Record your progress on Workguide page 5.

58-D. Spacing: double. Record your score.

58-D. SKILL MEASUREMENT: 3-MINUTE TIMED WRITING

13   By itself, the typewriter has brought about many major   12
14 changes in office routines, but at first it was not used in   24
15 an office. Mark Twain bought one of the first machines and   36
16 was the first one to turn in a typed manuscript for a book.   48
17   Court reporters were thought to be the main market for   60
18 typewriters. Next in order were lawyers and preachers. No   72
19 mention was ever made of the business use of the equipment.   84
20 Still, women seized the chance to enter an office by learn-   96
21 ing to type, and, as they say, the rest is history. Today,   108
22 typewriters and computers are the mainstay for office work.   120

I I I 2 I 3 I 4 I 5 I 6 I 7 I 8 I 9 I 10 I 11 I 12

5-B. BUILD SKILL ON SHORT SENTENCES

3 Vickie loved the fame she had achieved.

4 Save the three rolls of dimes for Chad.

5 Todd had sold a set of tires to Victor.

6 The old farmer deeded the farm to Eric.

5-C. BUILD SKILL ON WORD FAMILIES

7 fame tame lame same|lace face mace race

8 fold cold mold told|mail tail sail rail

9 feed seed deed heed|mate late date fate

5-D. MEASURING SPEED

5-D. After studying 5-D, complete Workguide page 14.

If you are using the keyboarding software, your speed will be computed automatically.

1. Type for an exact number of minutes while someone times you.
2. Find out how many "average" words you have typed. Every 5 strokes count as 1 average word as marked off by the horizontal scales and, in paragraph copy, as cumulatively totaled after each line. The first example below contains (8 + 8 + 2) 18 words.

Compare with line 12.

Emma races small cars at a short track.
Emma races small cars at a short track.
Emma races
| | | 2 | 3 | 4 | 5 | 6 | 7 | 8

The second example contains (24 + 4) 28 words.
3. Divide the words typed by the number of minutes typed. If you type 28 words in 2 minutes, for example, you type (28 ÷ 2) 14 wam (words a minute); in 1 minute, (28 ÷ 1) 28 wam; or in ½ minute, (28 ÷ ½) 56 wam.

Compare with lines 13–15.

Dale took Tom home to see David. David cooked a dish of fresh catfish for him. Dale served Tom his homemade ice cream. Dale took Tom home
| | | 2 | 3 | 4 | 5 | 6 | 7 | 8

5-E. BUILD SKILL ON SHORT SENTENCES

5-E. If you can be timed, take a 1-minute timing on each line instead of typing it twice. Compute your speed; circle and count errors.

10 Sara had five half liters of cold milk.

11 Rich visited Alaska after he left home.

12 Emma races small cars at a short track.
| | | 2 | 3 | 4 | 5 | 6 | 7 | 8 = 5-stroke words

5-F. BUILD SKILL ON A SHORT PARAGRAPH

5-F. If you can be timed, take two 1-minute timings instead of typing the paragraph twice. Compute your speed and count errors.

CUMULATIVE WORDS

13 Dale took Tom home to see David. David   8

14 cooked a dish of fresh catfish for him.   16

15 Dale served Tom his homemade ice cream.   24
| | | 2 | 3 | 4 | 5 | 6 | 7 | 8

5-G. SKILL MEASUREMENT: 1-MINUTE TIMED WRITING

5-G. Take three 1-minute timings. Try to complete both lines each time. Compute your speed and count errors.

16 Carla asked Vi Filmore if she liked her   8

17 red jacket. Vi said she did.   14
| | | 2 | 3 | 4 | 5 | 6 | 7 | 8

LETTER 21
PERSONAL-BUSINESS LETTER IN
MODIFIED-BLOCK STYLE

Paper: plain

November 19, 19--   3

Mr. Marshall Dixon, Manager   9

Customer Relations   12

Worldwide Airlines   16

2000 Cleveland Street   20

Dallas, TX 75215   23

Dear Mr. Dixon:

~~Gentlemen:~~   26

On August 15, 19--, I took Worldwide Flight 307 from Detroit, Michigan, to   41

Boston, (Mass). My ticket number was 437-0865, and my frequent   56

flier number ~~was~~ *is* 78228264.   61

~~Although~~ the flight was actually 632 miles, *but* I should have   71

recieved credit for 1,000 miles. *Page 2 of* Your sign-up brochure states   86

that all flights between 501 miles and 1,000 miles will   97

automatically receive credit for 1,000 miles. *Instead, I received*   110

credit for only 500 miles.   116

~~I am annoyed that this would happen.~~ Would you please correct   121

this error and give me credit for *#*an additional 500 miles on my   133

next account statement. *Thank you.*   140

                    Sincerely,   142

                    (Mr.) Leonard Plachta   145

                    8800 Lucerne Avenue   149

                    Detroit, MI 48239   153

MEMO 9
Paper: plain

This memo, dated December 1, 19—, is from Marshall Dixon, Customer Relations, to Harriet
Small, Billing Department. The subject is Customer Billing Error.   28

    Would you please verify that Mr. Plachta (letter en-   38

closed) is entitled to 1,000 miles for Flight 037, and if so,   51

credit him with an additional 500 miles on his next statement.   63

    I frankly do not understand how such an error could   73

occur. I thought all mileage was calculated by the computer.   85

If so, the only opportunity for error would be if the opera-   97

tor entered the wrong flight number. *Is that what happened?* ~~But that was obviously~~   109

~~not the case with Mr. Plachta.~~ Perhaps you can enlighten me.   116

After you check this out,   *to*   *nd explain*
~~If an error was made,~~ please write, Mr. Plachta a ~~letter~~   127

the situation   *also*
~~of apology.~~ It would be a nice gesture to give him a bonus   138

credit to help compensate for our error.   146

Closing lines?   149

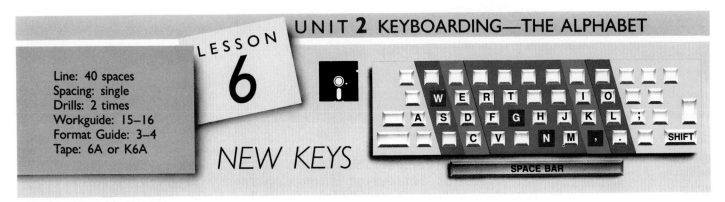

LESSON

6

NEW KEYS

Line: 40 spaces
Spacing: single
Drills: 2 times
Workguide: 15–16
Format Guide: 3–4
Tape: 6A or K6A

Goals: To control the N, W, comma, and G keys; to type 15 wam/1'/3e.

"15 wam/1'/3e" means to type at the rate of 15 words a minute for 1 minute with no more than 3 errors.

6-A. WARMUP

1 A market sold major food items at cost.
2 David sat at his desk for a short time.

6-B. PRACTICE THE N KEY

Use the J finger.

3 jjj jnj jnj njn jjj jnj jnj njn jjj jnj
4 not and tan tin kin den sin ran fan man
5 none then seen find cent even rain sane
6 Ann cannot enter the old main entrance.

6-C. PRACTICE THE W KEY

Use the S finger.

7 sss sws sws wsw sss sws sws wsw sss sws
8 saw few law who row wow how tow two now
9 wave saws wait warm wine when will want
10 Wanda will want to walk with Walt Shaw.

6-D. TECHNIQUE TYPING: SPACE BAR

11 Sam let Art do it. Fred drove to work.
12 Al is not in. Ed is in. Ed can do it.

6-E. PRACTICE THE , KEY

Use the K finger.

Space once after a comma.

13 kkk k,k k,k ,k, kkk k,k k,k ,k, kkk k,k
14 do, so, is, if, no, it, oh, to, of, or,
15 too, it is it, as soon as, if so, what,
16 Amos, Fred, Clark, and Daniel left too.

SKILLBUILDING AND CORRESPONDENCE REVIEW

Line: 60 spaces
Tab: 5, center
Spacing: single
Drills: 2 times
Format Guide: 47–50
Tape: 24A

Goals: To build speed and accuracy; to review the formatting of personal-business letters and interoffice memorandums.

57-A. WARMUP

S 1 The name of the rich old man in their town is Henry Dudley.
A 2 Thomas F. Barrows of Phoenix, Arizona, jogged very quickly.
N 3 We purchased a new Model 45 for $1,760 on October 23, 1988.

SKILLBUILDING

57-B. TECHNIQUE TYPING: SHIFT/CAPS AND RETURN/ENTER KEYS

Take several 1-minute timings. Try not to slow down for the capital letters.

Shift Key

4   Jim went to Iowa City, Iowa, in May to see Mr. Day. I   12
5 saw Jim at Big Joe's Deli on Oak Street on Monday. He said 24
6 the Blue Jays will play the Ink Blots on St. Patrick's Day. 36
7 If so, I will fly to El Paso on Key City Airlines with Jim. 48
  | 1 | 2 | 3 | 4 | 5 | 6 | 7 | 8 | 9 | 10 | 11 | 12

Type each sentence on a separate line. Do not slow down when you strike the return key.

Return Key

8 Who should go? Can you attend? Why not? Will Ann attend?
9 Someone should go. They need us. It won't take long. Ask
10 Ann to go. She may like it. Who knows? I can't go. I'll
11 be gone. If not, I'd go. Will you ask Ann? Thanks a lot.

57-C. PACED PRACTICE

Turn to the Paced Practice routine at the back of the book. Take several 2-minute timings, starting at the speed at which you left off the last time. Record your progress on Workguide page 6.

PRETEST. Take a 1-minute timing; compute your speed and count errors.

57-D. PRETEST: CLOSE REACHES

12   Did anybody try to stymie the enemy when he loaded his 12
13 weapon? Sad to say, all fifty of them had no choice but to 24
14 attempt to avoid more bloodshed by not making a loud noise. 36
   | 1 | 2 | 3 | 4 | 5 | 6 | 7 | 8 | 9 | 10 | 11 | 12

PRACTICE.
  Speed Emphasis: If you made 2 or fewer errors on the Pretest, type each line twice.
  Accuracy Emphasis: If you made 3 or more errors, type each group of lines (as though it were a paragraph) twice.

57-E. PRACTICE: ADJACENT KEYS

15 tr traded tragic sentry trace tries stray extra metro retry
16 po pocket poorly teapot point poise pound spoke vapor tempo
17 sa salads sanded mimosa sadly safer usage essay visas psalm
18 oi boiled noises choice oiled doing coins avoid broil spoil

57-F. PRACTICE: CONSECUTIVE FINGERS

19 my myself myrtle myopia myths myrrh enemy foamy roomy slimy
20 ft drafts soften thrift after often fifty lifts craft graft
21 ny anyone canyon colony nylon nymph vinyl agony corny funny
22 lo loaded blouse pueblo loans locks along color hello cello

POSTTEST. Repeat the Pretest and compare performance.

57-G. POSTTEST: CLOSE REACHES

6-F. PRACTICE THE G KEY

Use the F finger.

17 fff fgf fgf gfg fff fgf fgf gfg fff fgf
18 got leg get sag tag nag age egg rag log
19 gain wage gown grew wing rage grow sage
20 The old green gown sagged in the front.

6-G. Take two 1-minute timings; compute your speed and circle errors.
(**Note:** Beginning with Lesson 7, you will not be reminded to circle errors.)

6-G. SKILL MEASUREMENT: 1-MINUTE TIMED WRITING

WORDS

21 Wilma joined the team for the last five   8
22 games. The coach liked her skills.   15

| | | 1 | 2 | 3 | 4 | 5 | 6 | 7 | 8

LESSON
7
NEW KEYS

Line: 40 spaces
Spacing: single
Drills: 2 times
Workguide: 17–18
Format Guide: 5–6
Tape: 7A or K7A

Goals: To control the left shift, U, B, and colon keys; to type 16 wam/1'/3e.

7-A. WARMUP

1 Cora and Ed liked cats, dogs, and fish.
2 Evie jogged more than a mile with Walt.

To capitalize any letter that is on the right half of the keyboard:
1. With the F finger home, press and hold down the left shift key with the A finger.
2. Strike the letter key.
3. Release the shift key, and return fingers to home position.

7-B. PRACTICE THE LEFT SHIFT KEY

3 aaa Jaa Jaa aaa Kaa Kaa aaa Laa Laa aaa
4 Jed Ken Mel Kit Ned Hal Ira Kim Joe Lee
5 Jose Hans Mark Nita Iris Kate Hank John
6 Olga Hall went with Mike Lee to Kenton.

7-C. PRACTICE THE U KEY

Use the J finger.

7 jjj juj juj uju jjj juj juj uju jjj juj
8 urn sun lug sue jug due run rut cue dug
9 just hulk junk must hums sulk dunk nuns
10 Joe Uhl urged Hugh to ask Manuel Sturm.

56-E. CORRESPONDENCE REVIEW

LETTER 19
MODIFIED-BLOCK STYLE

Paper: Workguide 103

Arrange enumerations with the numbers at the left margin and turnover lines indented 4 spaces.

November 18, 19— / Mr. Ibrahaim Abo-Motti / 145 King Street / North 12
Pembroke, MA 02358 / Dear Mr. Abo-Motti: 19

We want to extend our thanks to you for taking your first trip as a 33
frequent flier on Worldwide Airlines. To show our appreciation, we are 47
pleased to provide you with two special free gifts: 58

1. One free upgrade to a first-class seat on any Worldwide flight you 72
take this year. 75

2. One free weekend (Friday and Saturday nights) at the Hartley Hotel 89
in Boston. By copy of this letter, we are authorizing the reservation 103
manager at the Hartley to send your room charges directly to us. 116

You need only 20,000 miles to earn a free ticket on Worldwide. You 130
are now well on your way to your first free ticket. Welcome aboard! 143

Sincerely, / Marshall Dixon / Customer Relations / *(Your initials)* / c: 153
Reservation Manager, Boston Hartley 160

ENVELOPES 7 AND 8

Paper: Workguide 104

Prepare two standard large (No. 10) envelopes for Letter 19—one in upper- and lowercase letters with standard punctuation and one in all-capital letters with no punctuation.

LETTER 20
MODIFIED-BLOCK STYLE

Paper: Workguide 105

WP Some word processing centers measure output (productivity) in terms of the number of strokes or lines typed per day. Some software programs automatically compute the number of strokes, words, or lines produced.

November 18, 19-- / Mrs. Ann Byrd, Vice President / 9
City National Bank / 204 North Hudson Avenue / 17
Oklahoma City, OK 73102 / Dear Mrs. Byrd : 25

On November 1, Worldwide Airlines added 33
Charleston, West Virginia, and Providence, Rhode 43
Island, to the list of cities we serve. 51

There will be two daily flights from 58
Charleston to Dallas / Fort Worth, with easy connections 69
to over 100 other destinations, including Europe 79
and the Pacific. Providence will have three 88
nonstops daily to New York with convenient 96
connections to over 100 Worldwide destinations. 106

Since you are a frequent flier with Worldwide, 115
we are sure that you would want to know of this 125
additional service. Complete details are provided in 136
the enclosed brochure. Welcome aboard! 143

Sincerely, / Marshall Dixon / Customer Rela- 151
tions / (Reference Initials) / Enclosure 154

ENVELOPES 9 AND 10

Paper: Workguide 106

Prepare two standard small (No. 6¾) envelopes for Letter 20—one in upper- and lowercase letters with standard punctuation and one in all-capital letters with no punctuation.

7-D. PRACTICE EACH ROW

Top Row

11 We were told to take a train to Westin.

12 There were two tired men waiting there.

13 Write to their hometown to inform them.

Home Row

14 Jake asked his dad for small red flags.

15 Sara added a dash of salt to the salad.

16 Dale said she had a fall sale in Elson.

Bottom Row

17 He can come at five for nine old canes.

18 Melvin came to vote with vim and vigor.

19 Val had nerve to come via a moving van.

7-E. PRACTICE THE **B** KEY

Use the F finger.

20 fff fbf fbf bfb fff fbf fbf bfb fff fbf

21 big job bag bin bit bid bow bun cab orb

22 back bend blew bunt bent bulb bask bush

23 Robb burned the big bag of bad berries.

7-F. PRACTICE THE **:** KEY

The colon is the shift of the semicolon.

Use the Sem finger.

Space twice after a colon; once after a period following an abbreviation.

24 ;;; ;:; ;:; :;: ;;; ;:; ;:; :;: ;;; ;:;

25 Ms. See: Dr. Roe: Mrs. Low: Mr. Uhl:

26 Dear Mrs. Jones: Dear Jack: Dear Nan:

27 Date: To: From: Subject: as listed:

7-G. SKILL MEASUREMENT: 1-MINUTE TIMED WRITING

7-G. Take two 1-minute timings; compute your speed and count errors.

WORDS

28 Dear Fred: Bev would like to take Beth   8

29 to a Jets game. She can come tomorrow.   16

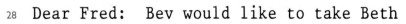

| 1 | 2 | 3 | 4 | 5 | 6 | 7 | 8

LESSON 56

SKILLBUILDING AND CORRESPONDENCE REVIEW

Line: 60 spaces
Tab: 5, center
Spacing: single
Drills: 2 times
Workguide: 103–106
Format Guide: 47–48
Tape: 24A

Goals: To type 40 wam/3'/5e; to review correspondence typing.

56-A. WARMUP

S 1 The busy girls kept their eight wigs in a box on the shelf.
A 2 Vince knew that Maxine just passed her formal biology quiz.
N 3 They spoke to 478 people on July 26 between 9:15 and 10:30.

56-B. PRODUCTION PRACTICE: ERROR CORRECTION

WP
To replace the word *kept* with the word *put* on a word processor, you would use the delete feature to remove the word *kept* and the insert feature to insert the word *put* in its place. The system would automatically move the rest of the line over to eliminate the extra space.

Spreading and squeezing are techniques used for making corrections that are shorter or longer than the original copy.
Spreading. To make a correction fill an extra space, move the word an extra half space to the right, leaving a space and a half before and after it. The best way to do this is to use the half-space mechanism (if your

machine has one) or to move the carrier by hand.
Squeezing. If an extra letter must be inserted, move the word a half space to the left, leaving a half space before and after it.
Practice. Type line 1 as it appears above. Then change the word *kept* to *put* and the word *wigs* to *gowns*. Do not retype the entire sentence.

> SKILLBUILDING

56-C. DIAGNOSTIC TYPING: ALPHABET

Turn to the Diagnostic Typing: Alphabet routine at the back of the book. Take the Pretest, and record your performance on Workguide

page 5. Then practice the drill lines for those reaches on which you made errors.

56-D. Spacing: double. Record your score.

56-D. SKILL MEASUREMENT: 3-MINUTE TIMED WRITING

4   Some students are quite shocked when they begin study-   12
5   ing about word processing to discover that some jobs can be   24
6   formatted quicker on a typewriter than on a word processor.   36
7   Is this really true?   40
8   Of course, it is. For example, think about formatting   52
9   envelopes. Their size makes it difficult to position these   64
10   forms in printers for printing. The same thing is true for   76
11   all business forms.   80
12   Likewise, short jobs that will never be revised should   92
13   be typed on the typewriter; in other words, you should make   104
14   good use of each machine by letting it do the types of jobs   116
15   that it can do best.   120

| | | 2 | 3 | 4 | 5 | 6 | 7 | 8 | 9 | 10 | 11 | 12

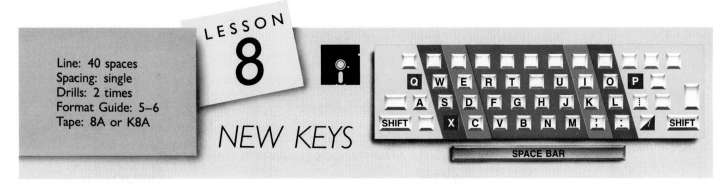

Line: 40 spaces
Spacing: single
Drills: 2 times
Format Guide: 5–6
Tape: 8A or K8A

Goals: To control the P, Q, diagonal, and X keys; to type 17 wam/1'/3e.

8-A. WARMUP

1 Wade bought Vi a jade ring at the mall.
2 Fred asked Merlin if Cora was at fault.

8-B. PRACTICE THE **P** KEY

Use the Sem finger.

3 ;;; ;p; ;p; p;p ;;; ;p; ;p; p;p ;;; ;p;
4 pan rip pat dip lip sip pen pad rap sap
5 page pale stop trip park palm peep pace
6 His pace kept him in step with Pauline.

8-C. PRACTICE THE **Q** KEY

Use the A finger.

7 aaa aqa aqa qaq aaa aqa aqa qaq aaa aqa
8 quip aqua quite quack equip quiet quick
9 quell quark quests quills quarts quotas
10 The quiet quints quilted an aqua quilt.

8-D. TECHNIQUE TYPING: SHIFT KEY

11 Elgin, Ohio; Sitka, Alaska; Ola, Idaho;
12 Mr. Ben Roth; Ms. Sue King; Ames, Iowa;
13 Mr. Vail; Miss Rubin; Mr. and Mrs. Mee;

8-E. PRACTICE THE **/** KEY

Use the Sem finger.

Leave no space before or after a diagonal.

14 ;;; ;/; ;/; /;/ ;;; ;/; ;/; /;/ ;;; ;/;
15 his/her him/her he/she either/or ad/add
16 do/due/dew hale/hail fir/fur heard/herd
17 Ask him/her if he/she and/or Al can go.

FORM 5
JOB-APPLICATION FORM

Paper: Workguide 101

WP   Printed forms, such as a job-application form, are most efficiently completed on a typewriter rather than a word processor. This is because it is difficult to adjust the printer to align the keyboarded copy with the guide words and printed lines.

It may be necessary to abbreviate some information on forms.

Remember: The line on the form should be in the position that a line of underscores would occupy.

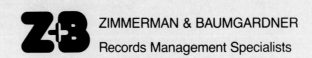

Z+B   ZIMMERMAN & BAUMGARDNER

Records Management Specialists

EMPLOYMENT APPLICATION

PERSONAL DATA
DATE __February 15, 19--__

NAME __Terry M. Martina__   SOCIAL SECURITY NO. __246-72-8480__

PERMANENT ADDRESS __145 Karluk Street, Anchorage, AK 99501__

TEMPORARY ADDRESS __Same as above__

TELEPHONE __(907) 555-3942__   MOST CONVENIENT TIMES TO CALL __1 p.m.-5 p.m.__

TYPE OF WORK

TYPE OF JOB DESIRED __Forms Secretary__   DATE AVAILABLE FOR WORK __May 19--__

WHICH OF THE FOLLOWING BUSINESS MACHINES CAN YOU OPERATE WITH COMPETENCE?

__X__ ELECTRONIC TYPEWRITER	__X__ DEDICATED WORD PROCESSOR
__X__ ELECTRONIC CALCULATOR	____ TELEX
__X__ MACHINE TRANSCRIBER	____ MICROFILM MACHINE

WHICH OF THE FOLLOWING COMPUTER SOFTWARE PROGRAMS CAN YOU OPERATE WITH COMPETENCE?

__X__ WORD PROCESSING	__X__ SPREADSHEETS
__X__ GRAPHICS	__X__ DATA BASE
____ TELECOMMUNICATIONS	____ ACCOUNTING

EDUCATION (MOST RECENT FIRST)

INSTITUTION	CITY/STATE	DATE GRADUATED
Federal Business College	Anchorage, Alaska	May 1989
Saint Vincent High School	Billings, Montana	May 1987

WORK EXPERIENCE (MOST RECENT FIRST)

COMPANY	CITY/STATE	JOB TITLE	DATES (INCLUSIVE)
Flynn & Lynch	Anchorage, AK	Typist/File Clerk	June 1987-Present
Better Burger	Billings, MT	Counter Clerk	May 1985-May 1987

8-F.   PRACTICE THE **X** KEY

Use the S finger.

18 sss sxs sxs xsx sss sxs sxs xsx sss sxs
19 vex box fox hex lax lux wax mix nix tax
20 next taxi apex flex flax text flux axle
21 Max coaxed six men to fix a sixth taxi.

8-G.   SKILL MEASUREMENT: 1-MINUTE TIMED WRITING

8-G. Take two 1-minute timings; compute your speed and count errors.

	WORDS
22 Jan packed her box with five quilts and	8
23 rugs. She had more but no plan to sell	16
24 them.	17

| | | 2 | | 3 | | 4 | | 5 | | 6 | | 7 | | 8 |

LESSON 9

NEW KEYS

Line: 40 spaces
Spacing: single
Drills: 2 times
Format Guide: 5–6
Tape: 9A or K9A

Goals: To control the hyphen, Z, Y, and ? keys; to type 18 wam/1'/3e.

9-A.   WARMUP

1 Susan packed two boxes of green grapes.
2 I have quit the marketing job in Idaho.

9-B.   PRACTICE THE **–** KEY

Use the Sem finger.

A hyphen is typed without a space before or after it.

Keep the J finger in home position to help guide your hand back after reaching to the hyphen.

3 ;;; ;p; ;-; -;- ;;; ;p; ;-; -;- ;;; ;-;
4 self-made one-third one-fifth one-sixth
5 ice-cold has-been show-off ha-ha tie-in
6 Ms. Ward-Smith was a well-to-do matron.

9-C.   PRACTICE THE **Z** KEY

Use the A finger.

7 aaa aza aza zaz aaa aza aza zaz aaa aza
8 zoo zap zig zip fez fizz jazz buzz daze
9 zest doze zing zinc zone zoom quiz gaze
10 The size of the prized pizza amazed us.

Line: 60 spaces
Tab: 5, center
Spacing: single
Drills: 2 times
Workguide: 101
Format Guide: 45–46
Tape: 23B

LESSON
55

JOB-APPLICATION PAPERS

Goals: To increase speed and accuracy; to learn how to type on a printed line; to format a letter of application; to format a job-application form.

55-A. WARMUP

S 1 What in the world did the visitors do with their idle time?
A 2 Do not jeopardize an equal tax by having Mack vote swiftly.
N 3 The 193 men and 287 women voted 264 to 216 for the $50 tax.

55-B. PACED PRACTICE

Turn to the Paced Practice routine at the back of the book. Take several 2-minute timings, starting at the speed at which you left off the last time. Record your progress on Workguide page 6.

55-C. TYPING ON A PRINTED LINE

Note: If you are not sure of the position that a line of underscores will occupy or how far above it the letters will print, type the alphabet and underscore it; then note the *exact* relation of the letters to the underscore and of the underscore to the aligning scale on your machine.

When typing on a lined form, adjust the paper so that the line is in the position that a line of underscores would occupy. (See note in left margin.)

To adjust the paper slightly up or down, turn the platen with your right hand while your left hand presses the variable spacer in the left platen knob. To loosen the paper for adjustments, use the paper release.

Practice 1. Remove your paper from the machine. Using a pen and ruler, draw four straight lines (each about 3 to 4 inches long) on the sheet of paper.

Practice 2. Reinsert the paper, and type your name in the correct position on each line.

<u>Peggy Wojcek</u>	Too high
<u>Peggy Wojcek</u>	Too low
<u>Peggy Wojcek</u>	Just right

55-D. JOB-APPLICATION PAPERS

LETTER 18
JOB-APPLICATION LETTER IN MODIFIED-BLOCK STYLE

Paper: plain

Tell what job you are applying for and how you learned of the job.

Mention the highlights on your enclosed personal data sheet.

Close by requesting an interview.

February 15, 19— / Personnel Director / Fairbanks General Hospital / 107 McKinley Drive / Fairbanks, AK 99755 / Dear Sir or Madam:

    I would like to be considered an applicant for the position of records assistant that you advertised in the February 13 edition of the <u>Fairbanks Courier</u>.

    I will receive my A.A. degree in Office Systems from Federal Business College in May. As my enclosed personal data sheet shows, I have taken courses in records management, computer software, and word processing. These courses would be especially useful in your medical records department. In addition, I have had office experience as a typist/file clerk for a legal firm.

    I would enjoy working as a records assistant at Fairbanks General Hospital. If you wish to interview me for this position, please call me at (907) 555-3942.

    Sincerely, / Terry M. Martina / 145 Karluk Street / Anchorage, AK 99501 / Enclosure

12
23
37
52
54
68
82
95
110
125
129
142
157
160
172
174

Elbow Control. Keep your elbows in close, hanging loosely by your sides. They should not swing out. Keep your shoulders relaxed and your fingers curved.

9-D. PRACTICE THE Y KEY

Use the J finger.

11 jjj jyj jyj yjy jjj jyj jyj yjy jjj jyj

12 eye yes yet yam joy you may way say ray

13 yarn year yawn yard holy fray eyed duty

14 Lazy Andy stayed in Troy to buy a ruby.

9-E. PRACTICE THE ? KEY

The question mark is the shift of the diagonal.

Use the Sem finger.

Space twice after a question mark at the end of a sentence.

15 ;;; ;/? ;/? ?;? ;;; ;/? ;/? ?;? ;;; ;?;

16 Can Ken go? If not him, who? Can Joe?

17 Is that you? Can it be? Who will see?

18 Did she ask? Can you go? Why not him?

9-F. TECHNIQUE TYPING: HYPHEN KEY

Hyphens are used:
1. To show that a word is divided (line 19).
2. To make a dash, with two hyphens (lines 20 and 23).
3. To join words in a compound (lines 21, 22, and 24).

19 Can Jerry go to the next tennis tourna-

20 ment? I am positive he--like you--will

21 find it a first-class sports event. If

22 he can go, I will get first-rate seats.

23 Zane--like Alice--liked to write texts.

24 Jill took Mary to a drive-in for lunch.

9-G. SKILL MEASUREMENT: 1-MINUTE TIMED WRITING

9-G. Take two 1-minute timings; compute your speed and count errors.

WORDS

25 Eliza landed a new job. She packed six   8

26 bags, quit her job, and moved away from   16

27 Michigan.   18

| 1 | 2 | 3 | 4 | 5 | 6 | 7 | 8 |

FORM 3
PERSONAL DATA SHEET

Line: 6-inch
Tab: 15, center
Paper: plain

List all items in reverse chronological order (most recent first).

If work experience is your strongest asset, list it first.

Include three references. (Be sure to obtain permission before using someone's name as a reference.)

TERRY M. MARTINA
↓2
145 Karluk Street
Anchorage, AK 99501
(907) 555-3942
↓3

Education

Federal Business College, Anchorage, Alaska
Degree: A.A. in Office Systems, May 1989
↓2

Courses in accounting, business communication,
computer software, machine transcription, office
procedures, office systems, records management,
typing, and word processing
↓2

Saint Vincent High School, Billings, Montana
Graduated: May 1987
↓3

**Honors,
Awards,
Activities**

Tuition scholarship, Federal Business College
Vice president, Office Careers Association
Member, Intramural Basketball Team
↓3

**Part-Time
Work Ex-
perience**

Flynn & Lynch, Anchorage, Alaska
Position: Typist/File Clerk
June 1987—Present
↓2

Better Burger, Billings, Montana
Position: Counter Clerk
May 1985—May 1987
↓3

References

Mrs. Susan M. Saifman, Instructor
Federal Business College, P.O. Box 1045,
Anchorage, AK 99506
Phone: (907) 555-7639
↓2

Mr. Robert N. Flynn, Attorney-at-Law
Flynn & Lynch, Route 4, Anchorage, AK 99509
Phone: (907) 555-3092
↓2

Ms. Elaine Harris, Principal
Saint Vincent High School, Billings, MT 59101
Phone: (406) 555-0992

FORM 4
PERSONAL DATA SHEET

Paper: plain

Prepare a personal data sheet for your own use in applying for a job.

Line: 40 spaces
Spacing: single
Drills: 2 times
Format Guide: 5–6
Tape: 10A or K10A

Goals: To strengthen all controls; to format paragraph copy; to type 19 wam/1'/3e.

10-A. WARMUP

1 Gwen Dunne expects too much from a job.
2 Keith had a very quiet, lazy afternoon.

10-B. INDICATING A NEW PARAGRAPH

See "Setting Tabs" in the Introduction, page xviii.

The word counts in this book credit you with 1 word (5 strokes) for each paragraph indention in a timing. Press the tab key after the timing starts.

When a paragraph is double-spaced, indent the first word 5 spaces. Use the tab key for this indention. Study the steps for setting tabs on page xviii.

When a paragraph is single-spaced, precede it with 1 blank line. The first word may be either indented 5 spaces or blocked at the left margin. (See illustrations below.)

Dear George:

    I would like to visit you next month. What plans do you have during June?

    We could go to Avon for a trip down the river. We had a good time last year.

Double-spaced, indented.

Dear George:

    I would like to visit you next month. What plans do you have during June?

    We could go to Avon for a trip down the river. We had a good time last year.

    Can you let me know how a trip like this sounds? A raft is a lot of fun, as you know.

Single-spaced, indented.

Dear George:

I would like to visit you next month. What plans do you have during June?

We could go to Avon for a trip down the river. We had a good time last year.

Can you let me know how a trip like this sounds? A raft is a lot of fun, as you know.

Single-spaced, blocked.

SKILLBUILDING

10-C. Spacing—single; tab—5. Take a 1-minute timing on each paragraph, or type one complete copy. Compute your speed and count errors. Use the tab key to indent.

10-C. BUILD SKILL ON SHORT PARAGRAPHS

	WORDS
3 Jenny asked if Alex had taken Vera	8
4 to work. She had planned to ask her to	16
5 ride to work.	19
6 Her car was in the M-Z Garage. It	8
7 needed to have one quart of fluid added	16
8 for the brakes.	19

| 1 | 2 | 3 | 4 | 5 | 6 | 7 | 8 |

Line: 60 spaces
Tab: 5
Spacing: single
Drills: 2 times
Format Guide: 45–46
Tape: 23B

LESSON
54

JOB-APPLICATION PAPERS

Goals: To type 39 wam/3'/5e; to format personal data sheets.

54-A. WARMUP

S 1 Both of the big firms in town also kept their workers busy.
A 2 Liz bought two very exquisite jackets from a downtown shop.
N 3 Pay Invoice No. 4036-B for $5,789.12 by 5:30 p.m. on May 2.

SKILLBUILDING

54-B. These words are among the 200 most frequently misspelled words in business correspondence.

54-B. PRODUCTION PRACTICE: SPELLING

4 using reason premium complete facility financial accounting
5 based recent receipt personal enclosed important successful
6 entry advise service eligible adequate equipment supervisor
7 means before absence security district receiving university
8 field annual support separate included completed authorized

54-C. Spacing: double. Record your score.

54-C. SKILL MEASUREMENT: 3-MINUTE TIMED WRITING

9   In order to make your writing clear to the reader, you   12
10 must keep each sentence short and simple. There is nothing   24
11 wrong with a thirty-word sentence so long as it is balanced   36
12 with some that are six, eight, or ten words long. However,   48
13 a short sentence that lacks other qualities of good writing   60
14 will have no use at all. Other good advice for a writer is   72
15 to emphasize common words and to use people as the subjects   84
16 of most of the sentences. This is how we talk, so the more   96
17 our writing sounds as though we were talking, the more eas- 108
18 ily our readers will understand what we write.   117

| 1 | 2 | 3 | 4 | 5 | 6 | 7 | 8 | 9 | 10 | 11 | 12

54-D. FORMATTING A PERSONAL DATA SHEET

At some point in your life, you will apply for a job. Generally, you will need a personal data sheet (or résumé), a letter of application, and a job-application form. You will prepare the personal data sheet in this lesson and the other two documents in Lesson 55. Since your job-application papers may create the first impression you make on the company, prepare them with care and accuracy.

A variety of styles is acceptable for formatting a personal data sheet. Choose a style that is attractive, and try to get all the needed information on one page.

10-D. ALPHABET REVIEW

Type each line twice.

9 Alma Adams asked Alda to fly to Alaska.
10 Both Bill and Barbara liked basketball.
11 Can Cass accept a classic car in Clare?
12 David did dine in the diner in Drayton.
13 Earl says Elmer edited the entire text.
14 Four fables focused on the five friars.
15 Gina gave a bag of green grapes to Gil.
16 Hal hoped Seth had helped haughty Hugh.
17 Irene liked to pickle pickles in brine.
18 Jody Judd joined a junior jogging team.
19 Keith kept a kayak for a trip to Koyuk.
20 Lance played a razzle-dazzle ball game.
21 Martha made more money on many markups.
22 Nan knew ten men in a main dining room.
23 Opal Olah opened four boxes of oranges.
24 Pat paid to park the plane on the ramp.
25 Quincy quickly quit his quarterly quiz.
26 Robin read rare books in their library.
27 Sal signed, sealed, and sent the lease.
28 Todd caught trout in the little stream.
29 Uncle Marty urged Julie to go to Utica.
30 Viva Vista vetoed the five voice votes.
31 Walt waited while Wilma went to Weston.
32 Xu mixed extra extract exactly as told.
33 Yes, your young sister played a cymbal.
34 Zesty zebras zigzagged in the Ohio zoo.

WORDS

10-E. Take two 1-minute timings; compute your speed and count errors.

10-E. SKILL MEASUREMENT: 1-MINUTE TIMED WRITING

35   Buzz expected a quiet evening with   8
36 his family. His sister, Kim, was to be   16
37 home from Java.   19

| 1 | 2 | 3 | 4 | 5 | 6 | 7 | 8 |

53-E. PRINTED FORMS

Although printed forms vary in size and style, well-designed forms enable the typist to use the margins and tabs to input most of the data. (See example below.)

1. The left margin is set at the first column. Tabs are set for additional columns.
2. Number columns (Quantity, Cat. No., Unit Price, and Amount) align at the right and are centered visually within the vertical lines. (Since the numbers are not uniform in length, set a tab for the most common number of digits and then either backspace or space forward for the other numbers.)
3. Word columns (Description) align at the left, 2 or 3 spaces after the vertical line. (Turnover lines are indented 3 spaces.)
4. The word *Total* begins at the start of the printed word *Description*.

Note: A purchase order is used by a company to order the goods or services it needs from another firm.

FORM 1
PURCHASE ORDER

Paper: Workguide 99

WP For forms that are used frequently in the office, some word processors can be programmed to stop at the first blank space, pause while you key in the variable data, and then automatically move to the next blank, pause, and so on.

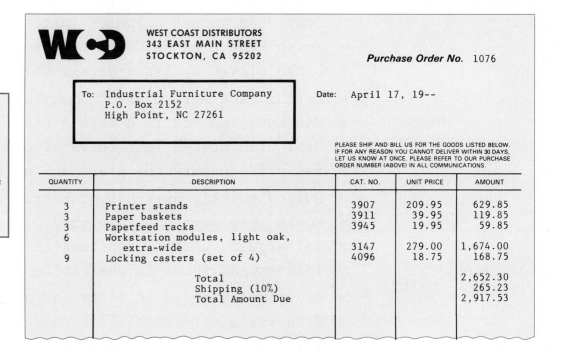

WEST COAST DISTRIBUTORS
343 EAST MAIN STREET
STOCKTON, CA 95202

Purchase Order No. 1076

To: Industrial Furniture Company
P.O. Box 2152
High Point, NC 27261

Date: April 17, 19--

PLEASE SHIP AND BILL US FOR THE GOODS LISTED BELOW. IF FOR ANY REASON YOU CANNOT DELIVER WITHIN 30 DAYS, LET US KNOW AT ONCE. PLEASE REFER TO OUR PURCHASE ORDER NUMBER (ABOVE) IN ALL COMMUNICATIONS.

QUANTITY	DESCRIPTION	CAT. NO.	UNIT PRICE	AMOUNT
3	Printer stands	3907	209.95	629.85
3	Paper baskets	3911	39.95	119.85
3	Paperfeed racks	3945	19.95	59.85
6	Workstation modules, light oak, extra-wide	3147	279.00	1,674.00
9	Locking casters (set of 4)	4096	18.75	168.75
	Total			2,652.30
	Shipping (10%)			265.23
	Total Amount Due			2,917.53

FORM 2
PURCHASE ORDER

Paper: Workguide 99

Purchase Order 1077, dated April 18, 19—, to Quality-First Computer Supplies, 1045 South Service Road, Plainview, NY 11803.

18 Data cartridges, 1/4 inch (Cat. No. 1980) @ 22.35 = 402.30

8 PC keyboard templates—MicroWord 3.2 (Cat. No. 8212) @ 12.95 = 103.60

9 Front-loading cartridges (Cat. No. 1840) @ 77.00 = 693.00

12 Space-saving copyholders (Cat. No. 6239) @ 34.95 = 419.40

Total = 1,618.30

Shipping/Handling = 243.00

Total Amount Due = 1,861.30

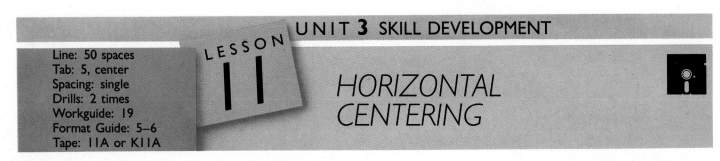

LESSON
11

*HORIZONTAL
CENTERING*

Line: 50 spaces
Tab: 5, center
Spacing: single
Drills: 2 times
Workguide: 19
Format Guide: 5–6
Tape: 11A or K11A

Goals: To type 19 wam/2'/5e; to center horizontally.

S = Speed

A = Accuracy

11-A. WARMUP

S 1 Jack went with Pam to the ball game last evening.
A 2 Fay quickly jumped over the two dozen huge boxes.

SKILLBUILDING

PRETEST. Take a 1-minute timing; compute your speed and count errors.

11-B. PRETEST: VERTICAL REACHES

WORDS

3 He knew about the rival races away from home 10
4 and ordered Gilbert to skip the seventh race. 19

| | 1 | | 2 | 3 | | 4 | 5 | | 6 | | 7 | 8 | | 9 | | 10

PRACTICE.

Speed Emphasis: If you made 2 or fewer errors on the Pretest, type each line twice.

Accuracy Emphasis: If you made 3 or more errors, type each group of lines (e.g., lines 5–8) as though it were a paragraph, twice.

11-C. PRACTICE: UP REACHES

5 aw aware flaws drawn crawl hawks sawed awful flaw
6 se seven reset seams sedan loses eases serve used
7 ki skids kings kinks skill kitty kites kilts kits
8 rd board horde wards sword award beard third cord

11-D. PRACTICE: DOWN REACHES

9 ac races pacer backs ached acute laced facts each
10 kn knave knack knife knows knoll knots knelt knew
11 ab about abide label above abide sable abbey drab
12 va evade avail value vapor divan rival naval vain

POSTTEST. Repeat the Pretest and compare performance.

11-E. POSTTEST: VERTICAL REACHES

11-F. Take two 2-minute timings; or type two copies. Compute your speed and count errors. Record your score on Workguide page 3.

11-F. SKILL MEASUREMENT: 2-MINUTE TIMED WRITING

WORDS

13 Zeke applied for the job some time last week 10
14 and was told to report to work this Tuesday. 19
15 Max would like you to help us locate a quiet 29
16 room with a sweeping view of the big harbor. 38

| | 1 | | 2 | 3 | | 4 | 5 | | 6 | | 7 | 8 | | 9 | | 10

Line: 60 spaces
Tab: 5
Spacing: single
Drills: 2 times
Workguide: 99
Format Guide: 43–45
Tape: 22B

LESSON
53

PRINTED FORMS

Goals: To increase speed and accuracy; to format printed forms.

53-A. WARMUP

S 1 A man named Chris laid his six keys down on the blue chair.
A 2 Jack Fox didn't place my big quartz vase in the top drawer.
N 3 Read pages 495-527 before 8:30 a.m. Friday for English 106.

SKILLBUILDING

53-B. All of these words are among the 125 most frequently misspelled words in business correspondence.

53-B. PRODUCTION PRACTICE: SPELLING

4 audit member faculty position addition insurance activities
5 basis amount whether customer property questions industrial
6 other review subject division decision following facilities
7 while return section possible mortgage corporate experience
8 areas either control proposal approval education electrical

53-C. PROGRESSIVE PRACTICE: NUMBERS

Turn to the Progressive Practice: Numbers routine at the back of the book. Take several 30-second timings, starting at the point where you left off the last time. Record your progress on Workguide page 5.

53-D. Compare this memo with Memo 8 on page 107. Type a list of the words that contain errors, correcting the errors as you type.

53-D. PRODUCTION PRACTICE: PROOFREADING

9 As called for in our recent agreement, an annual job perfo-
10 rmance appraisal will be conducted for all covered employ-
11 ees. Basically, the agreement requires each supervisor to
12 compare each employees' performance with established job
13 standards.

14 The purpose of the annual appraisal is to:

15 1. Document present job performance to provide management
16   with information needed to make decisions regarding salary,
17   promotion, transfer, and termination.

18 2. Aid in developing plans for improving based on agreed-
19   upon goals, strengths, and weaknesses.

20 4. Provide feedback on the success of previous training and
21   disclose the need for additional training

22 5. Provide the opportunity for informal feedback.

23 A joint labor/management committee is developing an evalu-
24 ation form that will be submitted to management for ap-
25 praisal. If you have any questions or concerns about the
26 new personal policy, please call me at Extension 1040.

11-G. Complete Workguide page 19 before doing 11-G.

WP

Word processors have an automatic centering feature that can center a line or group of lines without backspacing. They differ, however, in the *way* they center; that is, some disregard a leftover letter (as discussed and illustrated here); others do not.

11-G. HORIZONTAL CENTERING

To center words across the page:
1. Set the carrier at the center point of the paper (50 elite/42 pica).
2. Locate the backspace key in the upper right corner of the keyboard. This key is controlled by the Sem finger.
3. Say the strokes (including spaces) to yourself in pairs, pressing and releasing the backspace key one time for each pair of strokes. For example:

Br|uc|e |E.| E|dw|ar|ds

Caution: If you have a letter left over after calling out the pairs, *do not* backspace for this letter. For example:

Al|la|n |Le|ro|y |Fr|os| t

4. Type the words. They should appear centered on the line.

Practice 1. Center each of these names:

```
Toledo
Florence
Woodhaven
Osco
South Otter Creek
```

Check: The letter *O* aligns vertically.

Practice 2. Center each of these names:

```
Bruce E. Edwards
Martha Lee Donaldson
Allan Leroy Frost
Christopher Lakowski
Elizabeth Anne Webster
```

Check: The letter *S* aligns vertically.

Line: 50 spaces
Tab: 5, center
Spacing: single
Drills: 2 times
Format Guide: 5–6
Tape: 12A or K12A

LESSON 12

TYPING IN ALL CAPITALS

Goals: To type 20 wam/2'/5e; to type in all capitals.

12-A. WARMUP

s 1 Dad is going to bake two pies for you and me now.
A 2 Joe quietly picked six razors from the woven bag.

SKILLBUILDING

12-B. BUILD SKILL ON PHRASES

3 to do|you can|for us|at a time|do not|you will be
4 will have been|has been able|to be able|he is not
5 of this|in a|for me|you were|due to|for it|can be
6 will go|on the|with us|should have been|she and I

12-C. BUILD SKILL ON WORD FAMILIES

7 are fare mare tare bare care hare pare dare glare
8 end bend send mend tend vend lend fend rend blend
9 old told sold mold bold fold gold cold hold scold
10 ill till hill sill mill pill dill kill will still

52-D. FORMATTING MEMORANDUMS

MEMO 7
ON PRINTED FORM
Paper: Workguide 95

The abbreviation *RE* is sometimes used in place of the word *SUBJECT* in a memo or letter.

ENUMERATION. Treat each item as a separate paragraph with numbers at the left margin and turnover lines indented 4 spaces.

A copy notation on a memo is formatted the same way as on a business letter.

(TO:) Jileen Dagher, Shop Supervisor *(FROM:)* Evelyn Cunning- 9
ham, Human Resources Director *(DATE:)* October 19, 19— 18
(RE:) Performance Appraisal Form 23

Jileen, I've reviewed the draft appraisal form that your committee sub- 37
mitted on October 4, and I have these comments: 46

1. I suggest that you add a sentence under each category to help 60
explain what is meant. For example, under "Human Relations" you might 74
include this sentence: How effective was this employee in obtaining 88
cooperation, resolving conflict, and communicating with supervisors, 101
peers, and other personnel? 107

2. Add a summary evaluation, such as the following: "Indicate your 121
overall evaluation of this employee's performance, taking into considera- 135
tion the relative job importance of each of the categories above." 148

If your committee agrees with these two suggestions, I'm ready to 161
endorse your appraisal form and to seek the president's approval to place 176
the appraisal process into effect by January 1. Please let me know as soon 191
as your committee has acted. / *(Your initials)* / c: Legal Department 202

MEMO 8
ON PRINTED FORM
Paper: Workguide 97

(TO:) All Members of ASB Local 407 *(FROM:)* Evelyn Cunningham, 9
Human Resources Director *(DATE:)* October 19, 19— *(RE:)* An- 18
nual Performance Appraisal 23

As called for in our recent agreement, an annual performance appraisal 37
will be conducted for all covered employees. Basically, the agreement 51
requires each supervisor to compare each employee's job performance 65
with established job standards. 71

The purpose of the annual appraisal is to: 80

1. Document present job performance to provide management with 92
information needed to make decisions regarding salary, promotion, 106
transfer, and termination. 111

2. Aid in developing plans for improvement based on agreed-on goals, 125
strengths, and weaknesses. 130

3. Identify growth opportunities. 137

4. Provide feedback on the success of previous training and disclose 151
the need for additional training. 157

5. Provide the opportunity for formal feedback. 167

A joint labor-management committee is now developing an evaluation 180
form that will be submitted to management for approval. If you have any 195
questions or concerns about this new personnel policy, please call me at 210
Extension 1040. / *(Your initials)* 213

12-D. Make two copies. Copy 1: Type each sentence on a separate line. Copy 2: Type each sentence on a separate line, but tab-indent it 5 spaces.

12-D. TECHNIQUE TYPING: RETURN/ENTER AND TAB KEYS

11 It is now ours. He is. Ask her. Call me later.
12 Open the door. You can go. Let me see. He may.
13 Go for it. Right now. You can do it. Watch me.
14 You will. Giorgio left. He should. Write Mary.

12-E. PUNCTUATION PRACTICE

Space once after a semicolon and comma; twice after a period and question mark at the end of a sentence; twice after a colon.

15 Paul writes; Sam sings. Is it warm? It is cold.
16 Pat, May, and Jo like to read. Can Mike go? No.
17 I can go also. How is Kate? I will stay; hurry.
18 Did Jill go too? I hope so. Can William decide?

12-F. Take two 2-minute timings; compute your speed and count errors. Record your score on Workguide page 3.

12-F. SKILL MEASUREMENT: 2-MINUTE TIMED WRITING

WORDS
19   You briskly jogged exactly five miles taking   10
20 you past the gray dwelling that marks the zenith.   20
21   Jessie quipped that you cut five minutes off   30
22 your time due to the barking dog who lives there.   40
   | | 2 | 3 | 4 | 5 | 6 | 7 | 8 | 9 | 10

12-G. TYPING IN ALL CAPITALS

To type in all capitals:
1. Depress the shift lock on a typewriter or the caps lock on a computer.

2. Type the word or words.
3. Release the shift lock by touching the right shift key.

Practice.   Center each of these five lines horizontally. The letter *W* lines up.

MINNESOTA TYPEWRITING CONTEST
Held on Wednesday
FIVE BIG AWARDS GIVEN
Call John Wilbur Hall
WHITEWATER

Line: 50 spaces
Tab: 5, center
Spacing: single
Drills: 2 times
Workguide: 20
Format Guide: 7–8
Tape: 13A or K1B

LESSON 13

VERTICAL CENTERING

Goals: To type 21 wam/2'/5e; to center material vertically.

13-A. WARMUP

S 1 Joan can go to the show with Max if she wants to.
A 2 Mack Jacoby had a powerful zest for quiet living.

Line: 60 spaces
Tab: 5
Spacing: single
Drills: 2 times
Workguide: 95–97
Format Guide: 43–44
Tape: 21B

LESSON 52

MEMORANDUMS

Goals: To type 39 wam/3'/5e; to format memorandums with enumerations.

52-A. WARMUP

S 1 The eight men spent the day at work planting in the fields.
A 2 A few excited jackals squeezed by the open grove at midday.
N 3 My social security number (106-72-3854) was issued in 1967.

SKILLBUILDING

52-B. Change every singular noun to a plural noun. If you do so correctly, all lines will end evenly.

Change every plural noun to a singular noun. If you do so correctly, all lines will end evenly.

Change all first-person pronouns to the second person and vice versa; for example, change *I* to *you* and change *you* to *I* or *me*.

52-C. Spacing: double. Record your score.

52-B. CONCENTRATION PRACTICE

4   If the man, woman, and child want to vacate the old
5 apartment, the manager must issue the permit to make the
6 transfer legal. The tenant must approve the plan before
7 the vacancy or listing can be printed in the newspaper.

8   The managers asked the secretaries to type the letters and
9 reports that the officers had dictated earlier. When the jobs
10 had been completed, the secretaries consulted your assistants.
11 Your assistants discovered the errors and had the jobs redone.

12   You must give me your recipe for success in your profession
13 if I intend to follow you. If I become a broker also, you
14 can help me by giving me some leads and other contacts; you
15 could also have me subcontract a few of your small accounts.

52-C. SKILL MEASUREMENT: 3-MINUTE TIMED WRITING

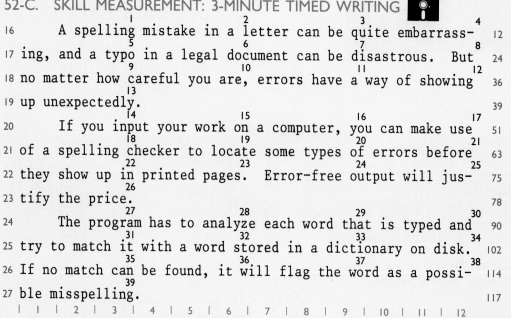

16   A spelling mistake in a letter can be quite embarrass-   12
17 ing, and a typo in a legal document can be disastrous. But   24
18 no matter how careful you are, errors have a way of showing   36
19 up unexpectedly.   39
20   If you input your work on a computer, you can make use   51
21 of a spelling checker to locate some types of errors before   63
22 they show up in printed pages. Error-free output will jus-   75
23 tify the price.   78
24   The program has to analyze each word that is typed and   90
25 try to match it with a word stored in a dictionary on disk.   102
26 If no match can be found, it will flag the word as a possi-   114
27 ble misspelling.   117

| 1 | 2 | 3 | 4 | 5 | 6 | 7 | 8 | 9 | 10 | 11 | 12

13-B. PRETEST: DISCRIMINATION PRACTICE

PRETEST. Take a 1-minute timing; compute your speed and count errors.

3   Opal alerted an astute older man to wear the 10
4 proper colored suit to the opera. His godson did 20
5 too. 21

13-C. PRACTICE: LEFT HAND

PRACTICE.
Speed Emphasis: If you made 2 or fewer errors on the Pretest, type each line twice.
Accuracy Emphasis: If you made 3 or more errors, type each group of lines (as though it were a paragraph) twice.

6 rtr sport train alert courts assert tragic truest
7 asa usage cased cease astute dashed masked castle
8 sds winds bands seeds godson woodsy shreds wields
9 rer overt rerun older before entire surest better

13-D. PRACTICE: RIGHT HAND

10 mnm hymns unmet manly mental namely manner number
11 pop opera pools opens polite proper police oppose
12 olo solos color lower locker oldest lowest frolic
13 iui fruit suits built medium guided helium podium

13-E. POSTTEST: DISCRIMINATION PRACTICE

POSTTEST. Repeat the Pretest and compare performance.

13-F. TECHNIQUE TYPING: TAB KEY

13-F. Set a tab every 10 spaces from the left margin. Then type lines 14–17, pressing the tab key after typing each word. Type each line twice.

14 dear TAB→ loan TAB→ care TAB→ idea TAB→ hike
15 your   quip   unit   name   four
16 item   zone   very   able   uses
17 same   lamb   etch   peel   year

13-G. ALPHABET REVIEW

18 aria bulb chic dead edge fife gage hash iris jive
19 kite lilt memo nine oleo plop quip rare skis tilt
20 undo veto waxy axes yoga zoom area bomb coca died
21 Jack Powell was quite vexed by such lazy farming.

13-H. SKILL MEASUREMENT: 2-MINUTE TIMED WRITING

13-H. Take two 2-minute timings; compute your speed and count errors. Record your score on Workguide page 3.

WORDS
22   Have you ever read the want-ad sections of a 10
23 paper? It is often possible to read of good bar- 20
24 gains. 21
25   In just a few lines of print you can read of 31
26 quality clothing, cars, prized gems, and pets for 41
27 sale. 42

51-G. FORMATTING A MEMORANDUM ON A PRINTED FORM

Although an interoffice memorandum can be typed on plain paper or letterhead stationery, it is often typed on a printed form with guide words, such as *To, From, Date,* and *Subject.* The forms may be either full or half sheets of paper, and the guide words may appear in different arrangements.

To format a memorandum on a printed form:

1. Set the left margin 2 or 3 spaces after the guide words; set the right margin to equal the left (by estimate).

2. Set a tab stop 2 or 3 spaces after the guide words in the second column.

3. Begin typing the insertions 2 or 3 spaces after the guide words, and align the insertions with the guide words at the bottom.

4. Separate the heading and the body with 2 blank lines.

5. Use reference initials and other notations.

To: George M. Dow General Manager	**From:** Patricia Hewson Media Relations	6 12
Subject: Accident at Site 5	**Date:** April 10, 19--	18

MEMO 5
ON PRINTED FORM

Paper: Workguide 93, top

WP — Because of the difficulty of aligning the heading data on a printer, printed forms are not used as frequently as plain paper for formatting memos on a word processor.

↓3

I have reviewed the technical reports from the chemical and   30
engineering departments and have also interviewed the operator   43
on duty the night of the accident. ~~Based on~~ On the basis of the information I   57
have on hand, I've drafted the ~~enclosed~~ attached press release.   68

Would you please review this release and make any changes you   80
feel are necessary. Station KXAR-TV and the Morning Herald   92
have already called to asking for our side of the story. ~~Thus~~ So 104
I would like to issue this press release as soon as possible.   116

↓2

wpr   117
~~Enclosure~~ Attachment   119

To: Patricia Hewson Media Relations	**From:** George M. Dow General Manager	6 12
Subject: Press Release	**Date:** April 11, 19--	17

MEMO 6
ON PRINTED FORM

Paper: Workguide 93, bottom

You have done ~~a masterful~~ an impressive job on the press release, Pat. I have   30
no changes to suggest at all. As soon as you have our ~~attorney~~ legal counsel   44
review it, you may send it out.   50

Perhaps you should set up a press conference for me on Wednesday 86
afternoon--early enough to make the evening news. My office has 96
also recieved several calls from the News Media, and I've   96
refered all inquiries to your office. Please let me have a list 101
of likely questions by Tuesday afternoon.   114
and suggested responses

pcb   115

13-I. Complete Workguide page 20 before doing 13-I.

WP   If you are using a computer with word processing software, you may use a *menu* to indicate the depth of the top margin. The vertical centering is then done either automatically or manually.

Also note that the copy in the practice exercises may not be centered exactly as described. It will depend on the word processing software you are using.

13-I. VERTICAL CENTERING

For material to look centered, the top and bottom margins must appear to be the same.

To center a group of lines and to provide for an equal top and bottom margin:

1. Count the lines (including blank ones) that the material will occupy when typed.
2. Subtract that number from the number of lines available on your paper. Most typewriters space 6 lines to an inch. Standard typing paper is 11 inches long.

Therefore, $11 \times 6 = 66$ lines on a full page or 33 lines on a half page.

3. Divide the remainder by 2 (drop any fraction) to find the number of the line, counting from the top, on which to begin typing.

Example: To center 5 double-spaced lines on a half sheet, you need 9 lines (5 typed, 4 blank); $33 - 9 = 24 \div 2 = 12$. Begin typing on line 12.

Practice 1. Center the material below on a half sheet. Double-space. Center each line horizontally. The letter *T* aligns vertically.

CITIES
Portland
Waters
Eastlake
Montrose

Practice 2. Center the material below on a half sheet. Double-space. Center each line horizontally. The letter *I* aligns.

APPRAISERS
Dunnings
Levine
Main
Pattison

LESSON 14

BLOCK CENTERING

Line: 50 spaces
Tab: 5, center
Spacing: single
Drills: 2 times
Format Guide: 7–8
Tape: 14A or K2B

Goals: To type 22 wam/2'/5e; to block-center material.

14-A. WARMUP

S 1 Joe has to stay at home today to take care of me.
A 2 Gaze at views of my jonquil or red phlox in back.

SKILLBUILDING

14-B. TECHNIQUE TYPING: SHIFT/CAPS LOCK

3 Her FOR RENT sign was run down by ROLLS TRUCKING.
4 Carpets ON SALE for this week ONLY--FREE PADDING.
5 Come see the TALKING BEAR. Certain to AMAZE YOU.
6 Add ZIP to your ad with OUR HELP. CALL ADS-RITE.

14-C. PUNCTUATION PRACTICE

Space once after a comma; twice after a colon.

7 The ties were brown, gray, and tan. I like them.
8 The list was as follows: milk, eggs, and cereal.
9 Jake wanted these items: books, pens, and paper.
10 We sit, read, and eat. They run, swim, and talk.

LESSON 51

Line: 60 spaces
Tab: 5
Spacing: single
Drills: 2 times
Workguide: 93
Format Guide: 43–44
Tape: 20B

MEMORANDUMS

Goals: To increase speed and accuracy; to format memorandums on printed forms.

51-A.   WARMUP

S 1 The girls with the keys may lay them down on the oak chair.
A 2 Tom quickly jeopardized his own life by giving the mixture.
N 3 The 10/23/89 invoice (#475) was for $132.86 plus $7.97 tax.

SKILLBUILDING

PRETEST.   Take a 1-minute timing; compute your speed and count errors.

51-B.   PRETEST: COMMON LETTER COMBINATIONS

4   At the conference last week, some person made a formal   12
5 motion that might be useful to us in the coming months. It   24
6 should enable us to easily comply with our building permit.   36
   | 1 | 2 | 3 | 4 | 5 | 6 | 7 | 8 | 9 | 10 | 11 | 12

PRACTICE.
   Speed Emphasis: If you made 2 or fewer errors on the Pretest, type each line twice.
   Accuracy Emphasis: If you made 3 or more errors, type each group of lines (as though it were a paragraph) twice.

51-C.   PRACTICE: WORD BEGINNINGS

7 for forget formal format forces forums forked forest formed
8 con concur confer conned convoy consul convey convex condor
9 per perils period perish permit person peruse Persia pertly
10 com combat comedy coming commit common compel comply comets

51-D.   PRACTICE: WORD ENDINGS

11 ing acting aiding boring buying ruling saving hiding dating
12 ble bubble dabble double enable feeble fumble tumble usable
13 ion action vision lesion nation bunion lotion motion legion
14 ful armful cupful earful eyeful joyful lawful useful woeful

POSTTEST.   Repeat the Pretest and compare performance.
51-F.   Tab: Every 11 spaces.

51-E.   POSTTEST: COMMON LETTER COMBINATIONS

51-F.   TECHNIQUE TYPING: TAB KEY

Alphabet						
15	Allen	Bates	Cohen	Drake	Evans	Fung
16	Gomez	Hogan	Innis	James	Kirby	Luke
17	Moore	North	Poole	Quinn	Reyes	Stan
18	Upton	Vogel	White	Xerox	Young	Zack

Number/Symbol						
19	$5.32	(451)	30.6%	18.3*	$6.84	#401
20	4,093	12:30	11'4"	5'10"	15/16	1.62
21	#3840	35-45	4:56*	3 & 4	5.42;	(4%)
22	11:50	(#47)	8.97%	$6-$7	23/24	#367

14-D. CONCENTRATION PRACTICE

11 The provocative statement caused an insurrection.
12 A congregation in Connecticut intervened quickly.
13 A lackadaisical traveler crisscrossed continents.
14 All resignations were interpreted as irrevocable.

Keep your eyes on the copy so that you do not lose your place as you type these longer words.

14-E. BUILD SKILL ON SHORT SENTENCES

15 It runs. Stand up. She works. Use it. He may.
16 Read the books. Come by. Drop it. Lay it down.
17 Pick him. Walk the dog. Watch the time. Go up.
18 Calm down. He likes it. You may not. They can.

Maintain an even pace.

14-F. SKILL MEASUREMENT: 2-MINUTE TIMED WRITING

WORDS

14-F. Take two 2-minute timings; compute your speed and count errors. Record your score on Workguide page 3.

19   The new girl on the block wants to study law   10
20 when she is out of school and to work for a large   20
21 law firm.   22
22   If she is a success, in seven years she will 32
23 expect to be a judge and quote from great lawyers   42
24 with zeal.   44

| 1 | 2 | 3 | 4 | 5 | 6 | 7 | 8 | 9 | 10

14-G. BLOCK CENTERING

To block-center a paragraph, center the longest line of the paragraph.

When several lines are to be listed, center them as a group, or a block:
1. Backspace-center and type the title.
2. Select the longest item.

3. Backspace to center that item, and set the left margin stop at the point to which you have backspaced.
4. Type the list, beginning each item at the left margin.

Practice 1. Block-center the display below on a half sheet of paper. Single-space. Leave 2 blank lines below the title.

PARTS OF A LETTER ↓3

Date
Inside Address
Salutation
Subject
Body
Complimentary Closing
Signature
Writer's Identification
Reference Initials
Enclosure Notation
Postscript

Practice 2. Block-center the 2-minute timing, 14-F, on a half sheet. Include the title *LAW CAREERS.* Use double spacing. Leave 2 blank lines between the title and first paragraph.

Practice 3. Block-center the display below on a half sheet of paper. Double-space. Leave 2 blank lines below the title.

RIVERS ↓3

Colorado
Hudson
Maumee
Mississippi
Missouri
Ohio

REPORT 17
TITLE PAGE

Paper: plain
Tab: center
Style as shown

If a report title or subtitle must be divided between two lines, try to have the second line shorter than the first, resulting in an inverted-pyramid appearance.

WP Some word processing software will let you select an option that will center the text vertically on a page when it is printed.

It is easy to determine the line number on which you are keying text on a computer for some word processing programs, because the line number appears on the screen.

↓13

THE SECRETARY IN TODAY'S AUTOMATED OFFICE

Maintaining Traditional Skills While
Developing High-Tech Competence

Line 33 ——→ Prepared by

Phyllis G. Browne
Systems Analyst
The Western Office Group

December 9, 19--

↑13

REPORT 18
TABLE OF CONTENTS

Line: 6 inches (60 pica/70 elite)
Tab: center

LEADERS. Use leaders (rows of periods) to lead the eye across the page. Always leave 1 space *before* and *after* the row of periods. (Spaces may also be inserted between the periods, but all leaders must align vertically.)

WP Some word processors have a leader-tab feature that automatically inserts leaders when the user is tabbing from one point to the next.

Note: For roman numerals that take more than 1 space, use the margin release and backspace from the left margin.

↓13

CONTENTS

↓3

I.   THE TRADITIONAL SECRETARY 1

      A. Training 2
      B. Hiring and Salary Levels 3
      C. Career Advancement 3

II.   THE MODERN SECRETARY 4

      A. Training and Experience 4
      B. Personality vs. Skills 5
      C. Career Paths 6
      D. Effect of Legislation 7
      E. Feminism, Chauvinism, and Sexism 8

III. CONTEMPORARY SECRETARIAL SKILLS 9

      A. Equipment Skills 10
      B. Administration Skills 12
      C. Technical Skills 14

IV.   LOOKING TO THE FUTURE 17

Line: 50 spaces
Tab: 5, center
Spacing: single
Drills: 2 times
Workguide: 21–22
Format Guide: 7–8
Tape: 15A or K3B

LESSON 15

SPREAD CENTERING

Goals: To type 23 wam/2′/5e; to spread-center material.

15-A. WARMUP

S 1 If you will call me, I will give you the new key.
A 2 The big quick lynx from the zoo just waved a paw.

SKILLBUILDING

15-B. BUILD SKILL ON PHRASES

3 which was|made up|came from|with them|about their
4 for a few|it can|speak up|all of you|in regard to
5 there are|as many as|it may be|if you can|into it

15-C. TECHNIQUE TYPING: SHIFT KEY

6 Joe Tao Sal Ann Yuk Sue Pat Jae Tab Fay Vera Rosa
7 Dick Fern Juan Mike Andre Fidel Pedro Chong Alice
8 Karen Ojars Marta Scott Carlos Maria Julie Ceasar

15-D. Take three 12-second timings on each line or type each line twice. The scale gives your wam score for each 12-second timing.

15-D. 12-SECOND SPRINTS

9 Jim cited the law to prove his case against Paul.
10 The unusual sights affected the men tremendously.
11 I accepted all conditions except this second one.
12 All the seniors played in the last football game.

| 5 | 10 | 15 | 20 | 25 | 30 | 35 | 40 | 45 | 50 |

15-E. PUNCTUATION PRACTICE

When you make the reach to the hyphen, keep the other fingers and the elbow relatively still.

13 Jan Brooks-Smith was a go-between for the author.
14 The off-the-record comment led to a free-for-all.
15 Louis was a jack-of-all-trades as a clerk-typist.
16 Ask Juliet--she's with Central Data--to find out.
17 Joanne is too old-fashioned to be that outspoken.

Line: 60 spaces
Tab: 5, center
Spacing: single
Drills: 2 times
Format Guide: 41–42
Tape: 19B

LESSON
50

SPECIAL REPORT PAGES

Goals: To type 38 wam/3'/5e; to format a report title page and a table of contents.

50-A. WARMUP

S 1 I wish to work with the busy chap who owns the eight autos.
A 2 Ken bought Mary five or six dozen pieces of quaint jewelry.
N 3 The 23 percent raise brought her 1987 salary up to $45,026.

SKILLBUILDING

50-B. PRODUCTION PRACTICE: PROOFREADING

50-B. Compare this paragraph with the first paragraph of Report 16 on page 101. Then type a copy, correcting the errors as you type.

4   The information processing manger is responsable
5 for providing support for the departments which are in-
6 involved in planning, installing, opperating, and main-
7 taining intergrated information-processing systems. These
8 systems may include word processing, electronic mail and
9 decicion-suppport systems.

50-C. SKILL MEASUREMENT: 3-MINUTE TIMED WRITING

50-C. Spacing: double. Record your score.

10   Some firms experience high turnover in their mailrooms   12
11 since jobs there are frequently low-paying. Thus, it is no   24
12 surprise that some firms have switched to machines to lower   36
13 costs. One new way to deliver mail inside of a firm is the   48
14 mobile mail unit. The unit is a self-propelled cart; it is   60
15 guided by an invisible path painted on the floor or carpet.   72
16 An electronic tracking system keeps the cart on track as it   84
17 zips up and down the halls. The cart makes regular rounds,   96
18 stopping at set spots to allow workers to remove their mail   108
19 and to insert mail for others.   114

| | 1 | 2 | 3 | 4 | 5 | 6 | 7 | 8 | 9 | 10 | 11 | 12

50-D. FORMATTING A TITLE PAGE AND A TABLE OF CONTENTS

Reports prepared for college or business often include a title page and a table of contents. The title page should appear centered horizontally and vertically. The information it contains may vary, but it always includes at least the report title, the writer's name, and the date.

The table of contents for a report should be on a separate page, with the heading typed in all-capital letters on line 13.

15-F. CONCENTRATION PRACTICE

18 The headmaster reprimanded an old procrastinator.
19 His mathematicians matriculated in Massachusetts.
20 An optimistic orchestra director was remunerated.
21 The ingenuous announcer was infatuated with news.

15-G. SKILL MEASUREMENT: 2-MINUTE TIMED WRITING

15-G. Take two 2-minute timings; compute your speed and count errors. Record your score on Workguide page 3.

		WORDS
22	Franz left out a vital model when he shipped	10
23	six big crates of new machines to the retailer in	20
24	a nearby town.	23
25	He was quick to see his error and made out a	33
26	new job order to send the extra model right away.	43
27	They were sold.	46

| 1 | 1 | 2 | 3 | 4 | 5 | 6 | 7 | 8 | 9 | 10 |

15-H. SPREAD CENTERING

To spread-center a line of type for greater emphasis, leave 1 space between letters and 3 spaces between words. To do this: back-space from center (*a*) once for each letter (except the last one) and (*b*) once for each space between words.
Practice. Spread-center these lines. Single-space. Leave 2 blank lines below the title.

C L A S S   R O S T E R   ↓3

C H E S S E M A N N
E S T I L L
H A S S B U R G
P A S T U R A N
S I P E

The letter *S* should align vertically.

15-I. CENTERING REVIEW

15-I. This drill reviews the skills you have learned in centering display copy:
  Vertical centering
  Horizontal centering
  Spread centering
  Block (list) centering

If you are using a word processor or a computer, you will want to take advantage of its automatic centering feature where appropriate.

Practice 1. Center the display below on a full sheet of paper. Center each line separately. Double-space. Leave 2 blank lines below the title.

ACCOUNTING TERMINOLOGY   ↓3

Account
Asset
Capital
Credit
Data and Information
Debit
Income
Liability
Value

Practice 2. Block-center the display below on a half sheet of paper. Single-space. Spread-center the title. Leave 2 blank lines below the title.

E D I T I N G   ↓3

Capitalization
Grammar
Number Usage
Omissions
Punctuation
Repetitions
Spelling
Typographical Errors
Word Division

THE INFORMATION PROCESSING MANAGER
By *(Your name)*

The information processing manager is responsible for providing support for those departments which are involved in planning, installing, operating, and maintaining integrated information processing systems. These systems include word processing, electronic mail, and decision-support systems.

PLANNING AND COORDINATION

A recent survey indicated that most IP managers spend about 15 percent of their time in planning and coordinating information processing systems.[1] They first obtain user input and gather other information on the requirements of data communication, including the kinds of applications needed as well as the storage requirements for data.

They must also research such areas as available software, networking capabilities, and license agreements. Prior to making any purchase decisions, the IP manager should also complete a facility impact study to determine power requirements, environmental factors, and other building considerations.[2]

If you must divide a paragraph between two pages, always leave at least two lines of the paragraph at the bottom of one page and bring forward at least two lines to the second page. Do not have a side heading as the last line of a page. Do not divide the last word on a page.

ESTABLISHING POLICIES AND PROCEDURES

As much as a fourth of the IP manager's time is devoted to establishing systemwide policies and procedures for the overall information processing function.[3] Policies and procedures must be established for data storage, equipment maintenance, and user priority. Also included in this function is the training program that must be an ongoing part of any effective information processing operation.

Reynolds best summarized the IP manager's responsibility when he said, "Any manager who devotes all his or her energies to purchase decisions and who neglects the thousand other, less glamorous, details, will surely live to regret that decision later."[4]

Endnotes go on a separate page.

NOTES

1. Neal Morningstar, "The IP Manager: Who's Minding the Store?" *MIS Journal,* January 1988, p. 153.

2. I-Ming Aron and Robert Aron, *Information Processing,* Bird's Eye Publications, Inc., Boston, 1987, pp. 385–386.

3. Morningstar, p. 155.

4. LeRoy Reynolds, *Administration and Supervision: Theory and Practice,* 3d ed., The University of York Press, York, Mich., 1988, p. 389.

Numbers in right margin: 25, 39, 53, 67, 70, 75, 88, 103, 117, 131, 143, 156, 171, 185, 198, 202, 210, 224, 238, 253, 267, 280, 289, 302, 316, 331, 340, 341, 355, 361, 374, 384, 388, 401, 416

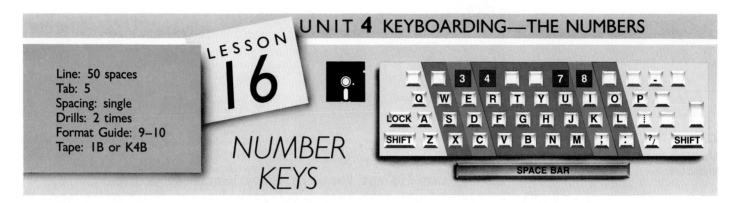

LESSON **16**

Line: 50 spaces
Tab: 5
Spacing: single
Drills: 2 times
Format Guide: 9–10
Tape: IB or K4B

NUMBER KEYS

Goals: To control the 4, 7, 3, and 8 keys; to type 24 wam/2'/5e.

16-A.   WARMUP

s 1 The small girl had a problem with the giant fish.
A 2 Packing jam for the dozen boxes was quite lively.

16-B.   PRACTICE THE 4 KEY

Use the F finger.

3 fr4f fr4f f44f f44f f4f4 f4f4 4 44 444 4,444 4:44
4 44 flakes 44 fans 44 figs 44 feet 44 fish 44 fins
5 The 44 pupils went to 4 different movies at 4:44.
6 The 44 adults were in charge of the 444 children.

16-C.   PRACTICE THE 7 KEY

Use the J finger.

7 ju7j ju7j j77j j77j j7j7 j7j7 7 77 777 7,777 7:77
8 77 jewels 77 jars 77 jets 77 jugs 77 jobs 77 jigs
9 Bus No. 7 made 7 stops and handled 77 passengers.
10 Joseph had 47 books, 74 magazines, and 77 videos.

16-D.   REVIEW THE 4 AND 7 KEYS

11 The 44 tickets were for the April 4 show at 7:44.
12 Anne was to read pages 44, 47, 74, and 77 to him.
13 When Jack turned 47, they had a party for 74 men.
14 Kate planted 44 tulips, 47 mums, and 74 petunias.

16-E.   PRACTICE THE 3 KEY

Use the D finger.

15 de3d de3d d33d d33d d3d3 d3d3 3 33 333 3,333 3:33
16 33 drains 33 dogs 33 days 33 dine 33 died 33 doze
17 The 33 boys had 33 books with 33 stamps in total.
18 If Charles adds 43, 44, and 347, he will get 434.

16-F.   PRACTICE THE 8 KEY

Use the K finger.

19 ki8k ki8k k88k k88k k8k8 k8k8 8 88 888 8,888 8:88
20 88 knives 88 kids 88 kits 88 keys 88 inns 88 inks
21 Flight 88 left at 7:38 and got to Boston at 8:38.
22 Please call Sue at 347-8833 or 847-3883 at 8 a.m.

ENDNOTES

Line: 60 spaces
Tab: 5, center
Spacing: single
Drills: 2 times
Format Guide: 39–42
Tape: 18B

Goals: To increase speed and accuracy; to type a report with endnotes.

49-A. WARMUP

s 1 The big man did not burn the ivory handle of the oak chair.
A 2 Because he was very lazy, Jack paid for six games and quit.
N 3 I got 98 of 147 items correct on the ENG 605 test at 12:30.

SKILLBUILDING

49-B. Take a 1-minute timing on the first paragraph to establish your base speed. Then take several 1-minute timings on the remaining paragraphs. As soon as you equal or exceed your base speed on one paragraph, advance to the next one.

49-B. SUSTAINED TYPING: ROUGH DRAFT

4   Buying office chairs is not as simple as it may sound.   12
5 Computer operators must now stay seated for long periods of   24
6 time and assume certain positions unique to their function.   36

7   The needs of these operators can not be met by the tra-   12
8 ditional office chairs. So Furniture makers now produce new   24
9 chairs designed to enhance the comfort of office personnel.   36

10   For a chairs to be comfortable, it they must have an adjust-   12
11 able seat. It must have the same contour of a typical human   24
12 body, and it must move in the same way that the body moves.   36

13   Seat height should must be adjustable so that there is quite very   12
14 little pressure on the legs when the feet are resting on the floor.   24
15 Chairs should also allow operators to shift in their seats.   36

| | 1 | | 2 | 3 | 4 | 5 | 6 | 7 | 8 | 9 | 10 | 11 | 12

49-C. ENDNOTES

Like footnotes, endnote references indicate the sources for statements cited. However, instead of placing the references at the bottom of the page, you type them on a separate page at the end of the report. To format endnotes:

1. Center the heading *NOTES* in all capitals on line 13.
2. Triple-space (leave 2 blank lines), indent 5 spaces, and type the reference number (not a superscript), followed by a period, 2 spaces, and the reference. Single-space the lines of an endnote, but double-space between endnotes.
3. Center the page number 1 inch from the bottom of the page.

↓13
NOTES
↓3

   1. "Software Leaves the Business Office," <u>Information World Weekly</u>, February 18, 1986, pp. 43-48.

   2. Jon N. Nicholas and Suzanne Rydahl-Fleming, <u>Winning Strategies for the Electronic Age</u>, National Policy Center for Voter Education, Washington, D.C., 1986, p. 179.

   3. Louise Plachta and Leonard E. Flannery, <u>The Desktop Publishing Revolution</u>, 2d ed., Computer Publications, Inc., Los Angeles, 1987, pp. 558-559.

   4. Terry Denton, "Newspaper Cuts Costs, Increases Quality," <u>The Monthly Press</u>, October 1986, p. 135.

16-G. REVIEW THE 3 AND 8 KEYS

23 Jack took the 8:38 train from Track 33 to Boston.
24 There were 838 men and 383 women at the 33 games.
25 On March 8 the 38 boys walked 8 miles to see him.
26 She added 3, 8, 33, 38, 83, and 88 to their bill.

SKILLBUILDING

16-H. Take a 1-minute timing on the first paragraph to establish your base speed. Then take successive 1-minute timings on the other paragraphs. As soon as you equal or exceed your base speed on one paragraph, advance to the next one.

16-H. SUSTAINED TYPING: SYLLABIC INTENSITY

27   There is no question that we have entered an   10
28 age of information. Many new processes and smart   20
29 equipment can now provide more data in less time.   30

30   The entire telecommunications industry has a   10
31 very bright future. With the use of the computer   20
32 and the phone, many data bases will be available.   30

33   The ease with which financial records can be   10
34 updated and revised is truly phenomenal. Visit a   20
35 nearby financial institution for a demonstration.   30

36   Inventory control has become simpler with an   10
37 emphasis on technology. Optical scanning devices   20
38 can help businesses with their inventory records.   30

   | | | 2 | 3 | 4 | 5 | 6 | 7 | 8 | 9 | 10

16-I. Spacing: double. Record your score on Workguide page 3.

16-I. SKILL MEASUREMENT: 2-MINUTE TIMED WRITING

39   The personal computer has affected the lives   10
40 of many people in the past decade. With software   20
41 programs appearing on a regular basis, people are   30
42 finding that the personal computer does help them   40
43 to do many long tasks in much less time.   48

   | | | 2 | 3 | 4 | 5 | 6 | 7 | 8 | 9 | 10

LESSON 17

REVIEW

Line: 50 spaces
Tab: 5
Spacing: single
Drills: 2 times
Format Guide: 9–10
Tape: 2B or K5B

Goals: To strengthen the manipulation of various machine parts; to type 25 wam/2'/5e.

S = Speed
A = Accuracy
N = Numbers

17-A. WARMUP

S 1 She hopes that they will have a good time in May.
A 2 Lazy brown dogs do not jump over the quick foxes.
N 3 Adding 43, 47, 73, 84, and 87 would give you 334.

Paper: plain
Visual guide: Workguide 59

WP   Many word processors have a special feature that enables you to position footnotes quickly and automatically, without having to determine where the divider line should go.

Note: As you type each superscript in the body of a report, estimate the number of lines needed for the corresponding footnote. Then place a light pencil mark in the left margin at the point where you should stop typing the text in order to leave enough room at the bottom of the page for the footnote.

USING MICROCOMPUTERS IN ELECTIONS *(TO WIN)*   7

Politicians throughout the country are *increasingly* turning to micro-   21

computers to help them run a more effective campaign. Comput-   33

ers have long been used for mass mailings and to help manage   45

campaign finances. Now they are *also* being used to help campaign   59

managers plan ~~winning campaigns.~~ *more effective strategies.*   67

For example, ~~it is estimated that~~ at least (10) different   74

software programs are available that contain maps with census   86

information.[1] The campaign manager can have a map with the   96

most recent voting patterns for each precinct appear on ~~his or~~ *the*   99

~~her~~ computer screen. Each precinct can be highlighted to show   122

the number of eligible voters, the number who actually voted   134

in the last election, and the distribution of voters ~~between~~ *among*   146

the political parties. Some software programs even allow   157

users to combine census and political data. Angela South Pick,   170

a Political Consultant who has used such a program, said, "For   182

example, you can ask to see all the areas in a district that   195

have at least voted 75 per cent republican over the past (4)   207

years and that have a ~~medium~~ *median* family income ~~of~~ between $40000   219

and $60000."[2]   221

  225

[1]"Software Leaves the Business Office," *Information World*   237
Weekly, Feburary 18, 1986, pp. 43-48.   244

[2]Jon N. Nicholas and Suzanne Rydahl-Fleming, *Winning*   255
Strategies for the Electronic Age, National Policy Center   267
for Voter Education, Washington, D.C., *1986,* p. 179.   277

Footnotes may also be typed with regular numbers followed by a period—for example:

1. "Software Leaves . . .

17-B. ALPHABET REVIEW

4 Jo quietly picked sixty sizes from the woven bag.
5 John quickly drew six zippers from the level bag.
6 Becky was amazed that Joe could quit giving help.
7 Pamela quickly fixed the valve for Jim and Buzzy.

17-C. NUMBER TYPING

8 Jeff was to read pages 37, 48, 74, and 83 to him.
9 The 7:38 bus did not come to our stop until 8:44.
10 Invoice 8 had ticket sales of 78, 44, 83, and 37.
11 We invited 43 boys, 48 girls, 7 men, and 8 women.

17-D. Type each sentence on a separate line.

17-D. TECHNIQUE TYPING: RETURN/ENTER KEY

12 Al won. Sheila lost. The team won. She forgot.
13 Will you go? Can he win? Who won? Where is he?
14 What speed did you reach? How accurate were you?
15 Tom will jog. Sue will bowl. Katie is swimming.

17-E. Set tabs every 10 spaces. Use the tab key to go from column to column.

17-E. TECHNIQUE TYPING: TAB KEY

16 You   should   be   able   to
17 use   the   tab   key   with
18 speed   and   control   without   looking
19 at   what   you   are   typing.

17-F. TECHNIQUE TYPING: SHIFT/CAPS LOCK

Use the shift lock when a word or series of words is typed in all capitals.

20 Review PAST DUE ACCOUNTS RECEIVABLE by AUGUST 10.
21 We will buy either a TOY POODLE or a FOX TERRIER.
22 Please R.S.V.P. to SUE KANE about the SHORE TRIP.

17-G. TECHNIQUE TYPING: SPACE BAR

23 a b c d e f g h i j k l m n o p q r s t u v w x y
24 is to go an it we if by in so at of or me and the
25 He is to be here as soon as he can buy a new bat.
26 You can buy a new boat with credit if you desire.

17-H. Spacing: double. Record your score.

17-H. SKILL MEASUREMENT: 2-MINUTE TIMED WRITING

27   Personal computers are creating a big impact 10
28 on all of our lives. We see them in the home and 20
29 on the job. Expect sizes and prices to change in 30
30 the future. Quite a change will also be noted in 40
31 the kinds of software programs that will be used. 50

| | 1 | 2 | 3 | 4 | 5 | 6 | 7 | 8 | 9 | 10 |

LESSON
48

FOOTNOTES

Line: 60 spaces
Tab: 5, center
Spacing: single
Drills: 2 times
Format Guide: 39–40
Tape: 18B

Goals: To type 38 wam/3'/5e; to format a report with footnotes.

48-A. WARMUP

S 1   Your major problem with the ivory handle is that it sticks.
A 2   Jack said Inez played a very quiet game of bridge with Rex.
N 3   Log on to Data File 89762 at 3:20 and log off before 12:45.

SKILLBUILDING

48-B. Take several 30-second timings on each line. Try to maintain the same speed on all these lines.

48-B. CONCENTRATION PRACTICE

4   It is up to you and me to do it if it is to be done at all.
5   Much of what they have said means that your plan will lose.
6   Conscientious secretaries transcribed their correspondence.

| | 1 | | 2 | | 3 | | 4 | | 5 | | 6 | | 7 | | 8 | | 9 | | 10 | | 11 | | 12

48-C. Spacing: double. Record your score.

48-C. SKILL MEASUREMENT: 3-MINUTE TIMED WRITING

7   Both at home and in the office, color affects the mood   12
8   and physical comfort of people. The decreased use of over-   24
9   head light fixtures in the modern office requires new color   36
10 patterns.   38
11   Red creates feelings of warmth but too much red causes   50
12 stress. Yellow is seen as cheerful, white will emphasize a   62
13 feeling of lightness, and blue or green look quite cool and   74
14 relaxing.   76
15   Just two or three colors should be combined in the of-   88
16 fice. Too many colors tend to look choppy. The colors you   100
17 choose for the office must reflect the type of work that is   112
18 performed.   114

| | 1 | | 2 | | 3 | | 4 | | 5 | | 6 | | 7 | | 8 | | 9 | | 10 | | 11 | | 12

48-D. FORMATTING REPORTS WITH FOOTNOTES

Footnote references indicate the sources of facts or ideas in a report. A superscript (raised) number is typed after the fact or idea in the body of the report, and the footnote reference is typed at the bottom of the same page. To format footnotes:

1. Single-space after the last line of text, and type a 2-inch underscore to separate the text from the footnotes.
2. Double-space, indent 5 spaces, and type the superscript footnote number and the reference. Single-space the lines of a footnote, but double-space between footnotes.

Note: When the last page of a multipage report contains a

> it does not make any difference."[1] Most newspapers formerly paid $25 per page for typesetting, but with the desktop publishing software, the cost has dropped to $8 per page.[2] ↓1
> ———————————————— ↓2
> [1]Louise Plachta and Leonard E. Flannery, The Desktop Publishing Revolution, 2d ed., Computer Publications, Inc., Los Angeles, 1987, pp. 558-559. ↓2
> [2]Terry Denton, "Newspaper Cuts Costs, Increases Quality," The Monthly Press, October 1986, p. 135.

footnote, the divider line and footnotes are typed at the bottom of the page—not immediately below the last line of text.

17-I. Center a double-spaced copy on a half sheet. Center each line horizontally. ·

17-I.   CENTERING PRACTICE

FALL FOLIAGE TRIP
↓3
Kittatinny Mountain Range
Saturday, October 8
Bus Leaves Parking Lot at 7 a.m.

LESSON
18

NUMBER
KEYS

Line: 50 spaces
Tab: 5
Spacing: single
Drills: 2 times
Format Guide: 9–10
Tape: 3B or K6B

Goals: To control the 2, 9, 1, and 0 keys; to type 26 wam/2'/5e.

18-A.   WARMUP

S 1 Is he to visit the client in Chicago or New York?
A 2 Quietly pack more new boxes with five dozen jugs.
N 3 Flight 374 will be departing Gate 37 at 8:48 p.m.

18-B.   PRACTICE THE 2 KEY

Use the S finger.

4 sw2s sw2s s22s s22s s2s2 s2s2 2 22 222 2,222 2:22
5 22 sports 22 sets 22 sons 22 seas 22 suns 22 subs
6 The 22 students in Room 222 sold all 222 tickets.
7 We will be there May 23 and 24 or June 27 and 28.

18-C.   PRACTICE THE 9 KEY

Use the L finger.

8 lo9l lo9l 1991 1991 1919 1919 9 99 999 9,999 9:99
9 99 lights 99 logs 99 lips 99 legs 99 labs 99 lads
10 The 9 boys and 9 girls in Room 9 sold 999 towels.
11 He got 38 pens, 29 pads, 74 pencils, and 9 clips.

18-D.   REVIEW THE 2 AND 9 KEYS

12 On 9/2 the group ate 292 hot dogs and 99 burgers.
13 You get 479 when you add 22, 29, 92, 99, and 237.
14 She had test scores of 92, 94, and 97 in English.
15 On 2/28 Michelle typed 29 wam with only 2 errors.

18-E.   PRACTICE THE 1 KEY

Use the A finger.

16 aq1a aq1a al1a al1a a1a1 a1a1 1 11 111 1,111 1:11
17 11 arenas 11 aces 11 axes 11 aims 11 arts 11 adds
18 Sam got 1,111 votes; Sue had 1,181; Vi had 1,119.
19 By 1991 he will have 17 new clients in 11 cities.

Use standard bound-report format.

Underline the italicized paragraph headings.

WP   Many word processors have an automatic page-break feature that provides the correct top and bottom margins on a multipage report.

Note: Never type a heading as the last line on a page. Also, if you must divide a paragraph between two pages, leave at least two lines of the paragraph at the bottom of one page and carry forward at least two lines to the next page.

RETAILING ORGANIZATIONS   5
The Last Stage of the Distribution Channel   13
By Kimberly J. Buckley   17

Retailers represent the last stage of the distribution channel that   31
goods follow on their journey from producer to consumer. Retailers   45
sell goods to the ultimate consumer for personal use. They merchandise   59
the goods using either in-store or out-of-store operations.   71

IN-STORE RETAILERS   74

In-store retailers use conventional store facilities, such as super-   88
markets or department stores, to provide goods for their customers.   102
They represent by far the largest category of retailers.   113

Independent Stores. An independent store is an individual retail store, 127
usually a small family-owned business. Most independents sell a rela-   141
tively narrow line of products, such as auto parts or records and tapes. 156

Chain Stores. A chain store is one of a group of similar stores owned   170
by the same company. The parent company normally buys products   183
directly from the manufacturer and distributes them to the individual 197
stores for sale to the final consumer.   204

OUT-OF-STORE RETAILERS   209

Out-of-store retailers do not use conventional retail facilities to sell 223
their goods. Instead, they rely on a variety of other promotional and   237
marketing techniques. Although both house-to-house sales and vending- 251
machine sales account for considerable volume, most out-of-store sales 266
are generated by either telephone or mail.   274

Telephone Retailing. In telephone retailing, salespeople call prospects 289
or follow up on the customer's response to promotional campaigns. In-   302
creases in printing and mailing costs, combined with new features pro- 316
vided by the telephone companies, have increased the use of this tech- 330
nique.   331

Mail-Order Retailing. Mail-order retailers ask buyers to order prod-   345
ucts from catalogs or from brochures sent directly to their homes or by 359
using order blanks placed in newspapers and magazines. Some compa-   372
nies distribute all their products through mail sales; others use catalogs 387
to supplement in-store retailing operations.   396

18-F. PRACTICE THE **0** KEY

Use the Sem finger.

20 ;p0; ;p0; ;00; ;00; ;0;0 ;0;0 0 00 000 0,000 0:00
21 100 parks 10 pens 10 pins 10 pits 10 pegs 10 pads
22 You will get 220 when you add 30, 40, 70, and 80.
23 The 20 employees should go to personnel at 10:10.

18-G. REVIEW THE 1 AND 0 KEYS

24 Mary read the 10 scripts and 11 texts in 10 days.
25 Please call her at 291-0011 or at 290-1001 today.
26 The 101 employees left at 10:11 instead of 11:01.
27 Raymond added 1, 10, 100, and 1,000 to get 1,111.

18-H. Spacing: double. Record your score.

18-H. SKILL MEASUREMENT: 2-MINUTE TIMED WRITING

28   We can expect quite a few changes in our job   10
29 market in the next few decades. People will have   20
30 jobs that will require new skills due to the many   30
31 uses of the computer. We will have a gain in the   40
32 size of the labor force, with more people working   50
33 in offices.   52

     | | | 2 | 3 | 4 | 5 | 6 | 7 | 8 | 9 | 10

LESSON
19

REVIEW

Line: 50 spaces
Tab: 5
Spacing: single
Drills: 2 times
Format Guide: 9–11
Tape: 4B or K7B

Goals: To improve speed and accuracy; to improve control of number keys; to type 27 wam/2'/5e.

19-A. WARMUP

S 1 The new worker had a small problem with the bank.
A 2 Jan quickly moved the six dozen big pink flowers.
N 3 Jeff got tickets 10, 29, 38, and 47 for the show.

SKILLBUILDING

19-B. PACED PRACTICE

Turn to the Paced Practice routine at the back of the book. Take several 2-minute timings, starting at the point where you left off the last time. Record your progress on Workguide page 6.

Line: 60 spaces
Tab: 5, center
Spacing: single
Drills: 2 times
Format Guide: 39–40
Tape: 17B

BOUND REPORTS

Goals: To improve speed and accuracy; to format a two-page report.

47-A. WARMUP

S 1 The usual visitor spent eight days touring the city sights.
A 2 Buz moved to Texas and plays rugby with Jackie quite often.
N 3 The lot at 8496 Circle Drive measures 107 feet by 235 feet.

SKILLBUILDING

PRETEST. Take a 1-minute timing; compute your speed and count errors.

47-B. PRETEST: HORIZONTAL REACHES

4   She thinks the chief hired a loyal agent for the extra   12
5 ship. He was alarmed at hints of terrorism. The agent was   24
6 armed and received valued input daily from all his sources.   36

  | | | 2 | 3 | 4 | 5 | 6 | 7 | 8 | 9 | 10 | 11 | 12

PRACTICE.
   Speed Emphasis: If you made 2 or fewer errors on the Pretest, type each line twice.
   Accuracy Emphasis: If you made 3 or more errors, type each group of lines (as though it were a paragraph) twice.

47-C. PRACTICE: IN REACHES

7 oy foyer loyal buoys enjoy decoy coyly royal cloy ploy toys
8 ar argue armed cared alarm cedar sugar radar area earn hear
9 pu pumps punch purse spurt input spurn purge pull spur push
10 lu lucid lunch lured bluff value blunt fluid luck lush blue

47-D. PRACTICE: OUT REACHES

11 ge geese genes germs agent edges dodge hinge gear ages page
12 da daily dazed dance adapt sedan adage panda dash date soda
13 hi hints hiked hired chief think ethic aphid high ship chip
14 ra radar raise raved brain moral cobra extra race brag okra

POSTTEST. Repeat the Pretest and compare performance.

47-E. POSTTEST: HORIZONTAL REACHES

47-F. PACED PRACTICE

Turn to the Paced Practice routine at the back of the book. Take several 2-minute timings, starting at the speed at which you left off the last time. Record your progress on Workguide page 6.

19-C. NUMBER TYPING

4 The 44 students bought tickets for the 4:44 show.
5 With 77 packets of thread, she made 777 sweaters.
6 Ticket No. 333 was entitled to 3,333 jelly beans.
7 She took Train No. 888 through 8 different towns.
8 Matt lived at 222 Lincoln with 2 dogs and 2 cats.

9 I threw only 99 pitches in the 9 innings pitched.
10 Gloria ran the 11 miles in 1 hour and 11 minutes.
11 When you add 10, 20, 30, 80, and 90, you get 230.
12 Order No. 2839 had 27 fewer crates than I wanted.
13 Call Robert at 724-3890 or 812-4410 for the data.

PRETEST. Take a 1-minute timing; compute your speed and count errors.

19-D. PRETEST: HORIZONTAL REACHES

14   The legal facts gave our lawyer a sense that 10
15 we had the upper hand. All written testimony had 20
16 impacted negatively on the young farmhand who was 30
17 being charged with several pyrotechnic incidents. 40

  | | | 2 | 3 | 4 | 5 | 6 | 7 | 8 | 9 | 10

PRACTICE.
Speed Emphasis: If you made 2 or fewer errors on the Pretest, type each line twice.
Accuracy Emphasis: If you made 3 or more errors, type each group of lines (as though it were a paragraph) twice.

19-E. PRACTICE: IN REACHES

18 wr wrap writ wren wreak wrist wrote wrong wreaths
19 ou pout ours outs ounce cough fouls dough coupons
20 ad adds dead wade adult ready blade adopt adheres
21 py pyre copy pyro pygmy pylon happy weepy pyramid

19-F. PRACTICE: OUT REACHES

22 yo yolk yoga your youth yodel yowls yokel younger
23 fa fact afar farm faith sofas fakes fades defames
24 up upon soup cups upset group upper super upsurge
25 ga gate saga gave cigar gains legal gasps garbage

POSTTEST. Repeat the Pretest and compare performance.

19-H. Spacing: double. Record your score.

19-G. POSTTEST: HORIZONTAL REACHES

19-H. SKILL MEASUREMENT: 2-MINUTE TIMED WRITING

26   Technology is making it possible for workers 10
27 at different sites to share more and more data in 20
28 less time. Experts tell us that by combining our 30
29 phones and computers we can have information that 40
30 will quickly zoom from one location to another to 50
31 help all jobholders. 54

  | | | 2 | 3 | 4 | 5 | 6 | 7 | 8 | 9 | 10

Provide an appropriate page 2 heading.

that the passenger is automatically enrolled in the air- 236
lines' frequent-flier program and is able to receive free 248
travel as he or she accumulates mileage on the airline. 259
There is no charge to join any of the frequent-flier pro- 271
grams. 272

Other services require that the computer user contact a 283
Travel Agent or airline to purchase the ticket. However, 295
the user can still be assured of getting the most convenient 307
or most economical flight by previewing the available 318
flights via a computer. 322

ON-LINE HOTEL RESERVATIONS 327

The Hotel Directory is another useful 335
on-line service available to computer 343
users. It provides up-to-date and com- 350
prehensive listings of more than 20,000 358
hotels worldwide. 362

Information Provided. For each of the 369
hotels listed, the program provides the 377
street address, the location (such as down- 386
town, airport, or ocean-front), the local 394
and any toll-free telephone numbers, the 402
number and types of rooms available, 410
room rates, credit cards accepted, and any 418
special facilities (such as health clubs, 427
heated pools, secretarial services, and the 436
like). 437

Access Procedures. Computer users 444
can search for a hotel by specifying a city, 453
the hotel name or chain, a range of room 461
rates, or the type of special facility de- 469
sired. If, for example, a city is selected, 478
all available hotels and motels in that 486
area will be listed. 490

19-1. Center a double-spaced copy on a half sheet. Center each line horizontally.

19-1. CENTERING PRACTICE

SEMINAR ON DATA COMMUNICATIONS ↓3
Featuring Dr. Albert B. Coleman
Professor of Business, Highlands University
Wednesday, October 18, 7:30 p.m.
Mountainview Resort
Highlands, Vermont

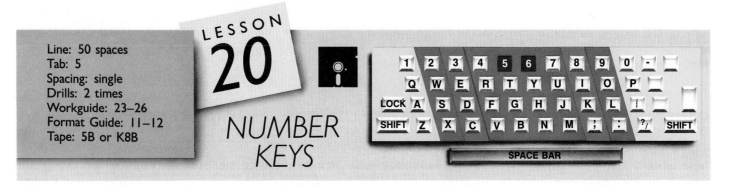

Line: 50 spaces
Tab: 5
Spacing: single
Drills: 2 times
Workguide: 23–26
Format Guide: 11–12
Tape: 5B or K8B

LESSON 20
NUMBER KEYS

Goals: To control the 5 and 6 keys; to type 28 wam/2'/5e.

20-A. WARMUP

S 1 They had problems with their profits from August.
A 2 Quickly pack the box with five dozen jars of gum.
N 3 Sue went from 380 29th Street to 471 27th Street.

20-B. PRACTICE THE 5 KEY

Use the F finger.

4 fr5f fr5f f55f f55f f5f5 f5f5 5 55 555 5,555 5:55
5 55 favors 55 furs 55 fads 55 fibs 55 foes 55 fury
6 The 55 students read the 555 pages in 55 minutes.
7 She found items 5, 10, and 29; I found 47 and 38.

20-C. PRACTICE THE 6 KEY

Use the J finger.

8 jy6j jy6j j66j j66j j6j6 j6j6 6 66 666 6,666 6:66
9 66 jewels 66 join 66 jabs 66 jump 66 jams 66 jots
10 At the age of 66, Tom moved from 66 Lincoln Road.
11 There are 53,640 people in Lodi; 28,179 in Alpha.

20-D. REVIEW THE 5 AND 6 KEYS

After doing 20-D, complete Workguide pages 23 and 24, the Punctuation Learning Guide.

12 The 65 adults went to 5566 Wooster Avenue on 6/5.
13 On 5/6 at the age of 6, Andrew weighed 65 pounds.
14 If Gail takes 10 percent of 650, she will get 65.
15 Call Jeffrey at 555-8407 or 555-5143 by 8:30 p.m.

46-D. FORMATTING A TWO-PAGE BOUND REPORT

If you do not have the visual guide for bound reports, make a light pencil mark in the margin an inch or so from the bottom of your paper to guide you in ending your first page at an appropriate point. Erase the mark later.

A bound report requires a wider left margin for binding. To format a bound report: (1) use the visual guide on Workguide page 60; (2) move both margins and all tab stops 3 spaces to the right. The first page of a two-page report is formatted in the same manner as a one-page report.

To format the second page: (1) Type the page number (without the word *page*) on line 7 at the right margin. (Do not type a page number on the first page.) (2) Begin the text of the report on line 10, a triple space below the page number.

```
                                        ↓7
                                      2 ↓ 3
                                        ↓
public grant, by will, by forfeiture, or by deed of conveyance.
There are two kinds of deeds in general use.

THE QUITCLAIM DEED
```

REPORT 12
TWO-PAGE BOUND REPORT

Line: 6 inches (60 pica/70 elite)
Paper: plain
Visual guide: Workguide 60

Determine where to end your first page in order to leave a 1-inch bottom margin.

REPORT 13
UNBOUND REPORT

Paper: plain
Visual guide: Workguide 59

Retype Report 12, this time in unbound format. Use your own name in the byline.

```
          COMPUTERIZED TRAVEL RESERVATIONS ] ds          6
                 By Miriam Caruso                        10

     Businesspeople can now use their personal computers to    21
make travel reservations.  They can search databases or hun-   33
dreds of thousands of flights in seconds to customize their    45
own travel schedule and save time and money.  In addition,     57
hotel reservations can be made on line.                        64


ON-LINE AIRLINE RESERVATIONS                                   70
     Using an electronic information service such as the       80
source or CompuServe, managers can identify flights through (and fares) 94
a special service operated by the air line industry; the       106
service will then display flights from it's more than 3        121
million records of available flights.                          124
     All of the information the on-line program needs is re-   134
quested from the user in question-and-answer format.  Users    146
must enter the location of thier departure and arrival ci-     157
ties, the travel dates, and the preferred times of depar-      168
ture.  The on-line program then displays all relevant          179
flights, including flight numbers, arrival and departure       190
times and fares. Some of the computerized reservation ser-     202
vices allow users to actually book their flights, paying for   214
them by credit card.  An added bonus of such services is       225
```

20-E. Take two 1-minute timings. Note that the last two digits of each number are a cumulative word count.

20-E. NUMBER TYPING

16 1101 1102 1103 1104 1105 1106 1107 1108 1109 1110
17 2211 2212 2213 2214 2215 2216 2217 2218 2219 2220
18 3321 3322 3323 3324 3325 3326 3327 3328 3329 3330
19 4431 4432 4433 4434 4435 4436 4437 4438 4439 4440

20-F. Take a 1-minute timing on the first paragraph to establish your base speed. Then take successive 1-minute timings on the other paragraphs. As soon as you equal or exceed your base speed on one paragraph, advance to the next one.

20-F. SUSTAINED TYPING: NUMBERS

20 In the past quarter, we have added the names 10
21 of 78 clients to our data base. This gives us an 20
22 exciting total of 249 clients in this first year. 30

23 Of the 249 clients, 91 were being handled by 10
24 Charles Thompson; 85 were controlled by Charlotte 20
25 Baines; and 73 were being serviced by Gail Banks. 30

26 We got 24 clients in July from 107 contacts; 10
27 August brought us 29 clients from 168 contacts; a 20
28 record of 35 clients was gained during September. 30

29 We were able to get 249 clients in our first 10
30 year; our aim is 350, 425, and 500 clients in the 20
31 next three years--or 1,524 clients in four years. 30

| | | 2 | 3 | 4 | 5 | 6 | 7 | 8 | 9 | 10

20-G. Spacing: double. Record your score.

20-G. SKILL MEASUREMENT: 2-MINUTE TIMED WRITING

32 The purpose for all the new technology is to 10
33 make workers more productive. If this happens, a 20
34 decrease in the number of hours on the job may be 30
35 noticed. This could mean that workers would have 40
36 extra time off. This could be quite a benefit to 50
37 a sizable number of employees. 56

| | | 2 | 3 | 4 | 5 | 6 | 7 | 8 | 9 | 10

20-H. Center a double-spaced copy on a half sheet. Spread-center the heading. Center each line.

20-H. CENTERING PRACTICE

ANNUAL FIREWORKS ↓3
Wednesday, July 4
Valley Road Park
Manchester, New Hampshire
Sponsored by Chamber of Commerce
Music starting at 7:30 p.m.
Fireworks beginning at 9 p.m.

LESSON
46
BOUND REPORTS

Line: 60 spaces
Tab: 5, center
Spacing: single
Drills: 2 times
Workguide: 91–92
Format Guide: 37–38
Tape: 16B

Goals: To use additional proofreaders' marks; to type 37 wam/3'/5e; to format a two-page bound report.

46-B. Spacing: double. Record your score.

46-A. WARMUP

S 1 Do not blame the eight girls who own the six pairs of keys.
A 2 A crazy dog was seen jumping quickly over a badly hurt fox.
N 3 Prices for new parts increased from 49% to 65% on 12/30/87.

46-B. SKILL MEASUREMENT: 3-MINUTE TIMED WRITING

```
          1            2              3           4
4     Most office workers find that some phase of their jobs   12
        5             6              7          8
5   relates to records control, no matter what their job title.   24
        9            10            11           12
6   Quite often, such duties take up as much as a fourth of the   36
       13           14           15          16
7   time for secretaries, clerk-typists, and accounting clerks.   48
            17            18           19          20
8       Regardless of the size of a firm or the type of record   60
           21           22           23          24
9   system that it uses, the job description of a records clerk   72
           25          26           27          28
10   will, of course, include the task of sorting and filing all   84
          29           30           31          32
11   kinds of letters, memos, or forms.  Records clerks may also   96
         33           34           35          36
12   set up coding systems and construct indexes or other cross-   108
          37
13   reference aids.                                             111
   |   |   2   |   3   |   4   |   5   |   6   |   7   |   8   |   9   |   10   |   11   |   12
```

46-C. PROOFREADERS' MARKS

The six most frequently used proofreaders' marks were introduced in Lesson 31. These six marks, plus 11 additional proofreaders' marks, are presented below. Study all the marks carefully and complete Workguide pages 91–92 before typing Report 12.

Proofreaders' Mark		Draft	Final Copy	Proofreaders' Mark		Draft	Final Copy
ss	Single-space	ss [first line / second line	first line / second line	*old* Change word		and ~~if~~ you	and when you
ds	Double-space	ds [first line / second line	first line / / second line	ℐ Delete		a ~~true~~ fact	a fact
¶	Make new paragraph	¶ If he is	If he is	... Don't delete		a ~~true~~ story	a true story
∩	Transpose	it is so	is it so	⌒ Delete and close up		co operation	cooperation
∧	Insert word	and it is	and so it is	≡ Capitalize		Fifth avenue	Fifth Avenue
V or ∧	Insert punctuation	if he's not	if he's not,	/ Use lowercase letter		our President	our president
# / ∧	Insert space	all ready to	all ready to	○ Spell out		the only ①	the only one
⌒	Omit space	court room	courtroom	⊙ Make it a period		one way	one other way.
				♂ Move as shown		no (other) way	no way

Ask your instructor for the General Information Test on Part 1.

PROGRESS TEST ON PART 1

TEST 1-A
2-MINUTE TIMED WRITING ON ALPHABETIC COPY

Line: 50 spaces
Tab: 5
Spacing: double
Paper: Workguide 27
Start: 6 lines from top

Let it snow. If those three words make your 10
pulse race, you probably like winter sports. You 20
may like to ski, skate, or sled in Vail. 28

The three words cause you to gaze quietly in 38
the distance as you don and adjust the right gear 48
for your expected trip to winter sports. 56

| | | 2 | 3 | 4 | 5 | 6 | 7 | 8 | 9 | 10

TEST 1-B
2-MINUTE TIMED WRITING ON COPY WITH NUMBERS

Line: 50 spaces
Tab: 5
Spacing: double
Paper: Workguide 27
Start: 6 lines from top

San Francisco has a public library system of 10
26 branches. The budget was over 13.2 million in 20
1986 for this 26-branch library system. 28

There are over 1,950,684 volumes in the sys- 38
tem and a circulation of over 2,695,510. Many of 48
the 712,753 citizens use the libraries. 56

| | | 2 | 3 | 4 | 5 | 6 | 7 | 8 | 9 | 10

TEST 1-C
HORIZONTAL AND VERTICAL CENTERING

Title displayed:
   Spread-centered
   2 blank lines
Line: center longest line; block-center listing
Tab: center only
Spacing: as shown
Paper: Workguide 29
Start: to center on half sheet

C R U I S E S

The Hill-Rowe Travel Company is pleased to
announce its annual winter cruises to the
Caribbean. The cruises include stops at:

          Antigua
          Barbados
          Grenada
          Guadeloupe
          Martinique
          St. Lucia
          St. Maarten

LETTER 16
MODIFIED-BLOCK STYLE

Date: current
Carbons: 1
Spacing: single
Workguide: 87

Enumerations within a letter are arranged with the numbers at the left margin and turnover lines indented 4 spaces.

ENVELOPES 5 AND 6

Workguide: 88–90

Type a No. 10 envelope for Letter 16 and a No. 6¾ envelope for Letter 17.

Mr. Jeffrey B. Baldwin   8

Baldwin's Department store   14

1732 Euclid Avenue East   18

Des Moines, IA 50313   22

Dear Mr. Baldwin: 26

I am happy to report ~~that many~~ *on several* developments *that* have occured since   40

you wrote *to* inquiring *e* about our newest sportswear line: 50

1. ~~Several~~ fabric *s* (sample) ~~pieces, as well as~~ *and* copies of our   58

     new catalogs were sent *n* last friday.   65

2. Application forms for a 30-day open charge account have *also*   78

     been mailed to you. As soon as these forms ~~have been~~ *are returned to us and* pro-   92

     cessed, we can begin ~~begin~~ sending you the latest in mens'   102

     and women's sports wear.   107

I have just learned that   *If you are available, I would like*

3. I will be visiting your area during the next two weeks, to   132

     show you some of our latest styles.   139

As soon as my travel plans are finalized, I will call you to   151

set up an appointment. *with you* I look forward to meeting you.   164

         Sincerely yours,

         Frazier T. Moen   170

         Sales Representative   174

evy   174

c: Ms. Gloria S. Berg   179

LETTER 17
MODIFIED-BLOCK STYLE

Carbons: 1
Workguide: 89

ENUMERATION. Treat each numbered item as a separate paragraph with numbers at the left margin and turnover lines indented 4 spaces.

(Current date) / Mr. Timothy J. Dickinson / Commercial Loan Department / Union National Bank / 7232 Hokulani Street / Honolulu, HI 96825/ Dear Mr. Dickinson: 13, 25, 29

The following information is provided as a follow-up to my earlier loan application form on behalf of Mid-Way Fabricators: 1. Mid-Way was founded by Mr. Alvin R. Chong in 1965. 2. Detailed itemizations of current assets and liabilities are provided on the enclosed balance sheet dated June 30, 19—, the end of our last fiscal period. 3. An income statement is provided for the same fiscal period.   44, 57, 71, 85, 99, 109

I look forward to seeing you on *(one week from today)*.   119

Sincerely yours, / Eileen F. Blanchard / Treasurer / *(Your initials)* / Enclosures 2 / c: Donald B. Taylor   128, 135

TEST 1-D
BLOCK CENTERING

Title displayed:
  Centered
  2 blank lines
Line: to center longest item
Tab: center
Spacing: single
Paper: Workguide 29
Start: to center on half sheet

MODERN U.S. SUSPENSION BRIDGES

Bronx-Whitestone
Delaware Memorial
Gas Pipe Line
George Washington
Golden Gate
Mackinac Straits
Seaway Skyway
Tacoma Narrows
Transbay
Verrazano-Narrows

TEST 1-E
LINE CENTERING

Title displayed:
  Centered
  2 blank lines
Line: center each line
         horizontally
Tab: center
Spacing: double
Paper: Workguide 31
Start: to center on half sheet

FOREIGN EXCHANGE

British Pound

Canadian Dollar

French Franc

German Mark

Japanese Yen

Mexican Peso

Swiss Franc

TEST 1-F
BLOCK CENTERING

Title displayed:
  Spread-centered
  2 blank lines
Line: to center longest item
Tab: center
Spacing: single
Paper: Workguide 31
Start: to center on half sheet

TEN LARGEST U.S. CITIES

New York
Los Angeles
Chicago
Houston
Philadelphia
Detroit
Dallas
San Antonio
Phoenix
San Francisco

Line: 60 spaces
Tab: center
Spacing: single
Drills: 2 times
Workguide: 87–90
Format Guide: 35–38

LESSON 45

LETTERS WITH COPIES

Goals: To improve speed and accuracy; to prepare letters with carbon copies; to correct errors on carbon copies.

45-A. WARMUP

S 1 Eight of their girls may take the big van when they can go.
A 2 Liz fixed Vivian's car; it goes quickly with jumper cables.
N 3 Panian had 1,209 votes, Smythe had 734, and Nelson had 658.

SKILLBUILDING

45-B. PACED PRACTICE

Turn to the Paced Practice routine at the back of the book. Take several 2-minute timings, starting at the speed at which you left off the last time. Record your progress on Workguide page 6.

45-C. CARBON COPIES

It is good business practice to keep a copy of all typed materials, either in the form of a *hard copy* (paper copy) in the files or in the form of *soft copy* that is stored in the computer or on a disk. A copy may also be sent to one or more individuals other than the addressed party. Copies can be made by typing with carbon paper, by printing out a second original copy on the printer, or by using a photocopy machine. Whatever method is used, indicate on the original document that copies have been sent to others. Follow the steps below for making carbon copies.

1. Assemble the carbon pack: *(a)* the sheet of paper on which you will type, *(b)* the carbon paper (shiny side down), and *(c)* the onionskin or other thin sheet of paper on which you wish to make the copy.
2. Insert the carbon pack into the typewriter: *(a)* Straighten the sides and top. *(b)* Insert the pack into the machine with the carbon side (and the copy paper) facing you. *(c)* Hold the pack with one hand, and use the automatic paper feed with the other. *(d)* Before you start to type, check to be sure that the letterhead or top sheet, as well as the dull side of the carbon paper, is facing you. Note: When using an electric typewriter, hold the paper pack in the left hand and turn the platen knob with the right.
3. To make corrections on carbon copies: *(a)* Use a soft (pencil) eraser to erase errors on the copy paper. *(b)* Place a stiff card under the sheet on which you erase to keep smudges from appearing on the copies beneath. (If you find an error after removing your paper, erase and correct on each sheet separately.)

WP On a word processor, additional copies can be made by (1) inserting a carbon pack into the printer (the piece of equipment that actually types out what has been entered on the word processor) or (2) having the system print out as many copies of the document as needed.

A copy (*c*) notation is added to a letter if someone is to get a copy of it. Type a small letter *c* on the line below the reference initials (or below the enclosure notation if there is one).

```
                                  Sincerely yours,


                                  Pat Dorf, Director

        slk
        c:  Barbara J. Reeder
```

PART 2

SKILLBUILDING■ LETTERS, REPORTS, AND TABLES

OBJECTIVES

KEYBOARDING SKILL

To operate the entire keyboard by touch.

To type 36 words a minute on a 3-minute timed writing with no more than 5 errors.

PROOFREADING SKILL

To proofread typewritten material, mark and count errors, correct errors, and compute typing speed.

TECHNICAL SKILL

To answer correctly at least 90 percent of the questions on an objective test.

FORMATTING SKILL

To make correct word divisions and line-ending decisions.

To format business letters and personal-business letters.

To format one-page reports, enumerations, and bibliographies.

To format tables with column headings.

■ To understand how word processing equipment and software would function if used to format various production assignments.

44-F. FOLDING LETTERS

To fold a letter for a large (No. 10) envelope:
1. Fold up the bottom third of the letter.
2. Fold the top third down to ½ inch from the first crease.
3. Insert the last crease into the envelope first, with the flap facing up.

To fold a letter for a small (No. 6¾) envelope:
1. Fold up the bottom half to ½ inch from the top.
2. Fold the right third over to the left.
3. Fold the left third over to ½ inch from the right crease.
4. Insert the last crease into the envelope first, with the flap facing up.

LETTER 15
MODIFIED-BLOCK STYLE

Paper: Workguide 85

Use the current date and your own reference initials.

Mr. Alvin S. Gumbel — 4
Assistant Manager — 7
Diplomat Hotel — 10
823 North Michigan Avenue — 15
Chicago, IL 60611 — 18

Dear Mr. Gumbel: — 22

We are pleased that you will be able to handle the — 32
arrangements for our annual convention to be held at — 42
your hotel from March 16 through 19. — 50

From our perspective, the preliminary meeting with you — 61
last week went very well. Our tentative convention — 71
program will be ready in about two weeks. — 79

With the professional assistance of you and your staff, — 90
we look forward to the best convention ever. — 99

Sincerely, — 101

ENVELOPE 4

Paper: Workguide 86

Type a No. 10 envelope for Letter 15.

Harold R. Ottoson — 105
President - Elect — 108

SYMBOLS AND WORD DIVISION

Line: 60 spaces
Tab: 5
Spacing: single
Drills: 2 times
Format Guide: 11–12
Tape: 6B or K9B

Goals: To control the **#**, **(**, and **)** keys; to improve speed and accuracy; to make correct word-division decisions.

21-A. WARMUP

S 1 The man took the keys that he had in his hand to the truck.
A 2 The four women in the jury box quickly spotted Dave dozing.
N 3 Seats 10, 29, 38, 47, and 56 are still unsold for tomorrow.

 NUMBER (if before a figure) or POUNDS (if after a figure) is the shift of 3. Use the D finger.

21-B. PRACTICE THE # KEY

4 ded de3d d3d d3#d d3#d d##d d##d #3 #33 #38 #383 #3,383 d#d
5 I want 33# of #200, 37# of #300, and 38# of #400 by Friday.
6 Package #47 weighs 65#; #51 weighs 84#; and #83 weighs 42#.
7 My favorite tours for this year are #29, #38, #47, and #56.

PARENTHESES are the shifts of 9 and 0. Use the L and Sem fingers.

21-C. PRACTICE THE (AND) KEYS

8 1091 191 19(1 1(1 1(1 ;p0; ;0; ;0); ;); ;); (2) (4) (6) (8)
9 Please ask (1) Tom, (2) Pat, (3) Anne, (4) Sue, and (5) Ed.
10 David brought some (1) skis, (2) sleds, and (3) ice skates.
11 The typist is (1) speedy, (2) accurate, and (3) productive.

12 Three of our workers (Parks, Lemay, and Eng) were rewarded.
13 The manager (Ms. Holden) went to Albany on Friday (June 5).
14 The man from Illinois (Mr. Roberts) will vote yes (not no).
15 My bingo is (1) B5, (2) I21, (3) N36, (4) G54, and (5) O73.

SKILLBUILDING

21-D. NUMBER TYPING

16 On the cruise ship Sunup, Cabins 20 and 19 were very small.
17 I know a man who is 21; his aunt is also 21; his dad is 60.
18 The tour had 874 people, 387 from Hope and 487 from Bangor.
19 We ordered 90 cartons and 43 boxes when we called 555-5536.

21-E. PRODUCTION PRACTICE: PROOFREADING

21-E. Compare these two paragraphs with the first two paragraphs of the timed writing in 22-J on page 40. Type a list of the words that contain errors, correcting the errors as you type.

20   Jobs in busness require good comunication skills for
21 sucess. Confirmation of this fact can be found in various
22 magzines and books.

23   It is expected that a new worker on business will have
24 the ability to speak and write clear and properly. These
25 are critcal skills.

44-E. FORMATTING ENVELOPES

Note: The format used for addressing this large envelope is recommended by the U.S. Postal Service for bulk mail that will be sorted by an electronic scanning device. The address is typed in all-capital letters with no punctuation, and it also incorporates the nine-digit ZIP Code. Either format illustrated is acceptable for first-class mail.

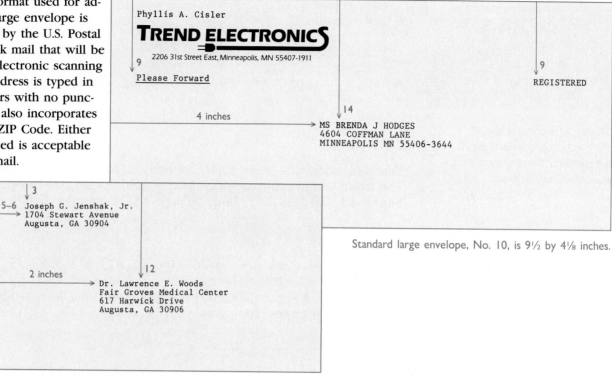

Phyllis A. Cisler

TREND ELECTRONICS

2206 31st Street East, Minneapolis, MN 55407-1911

9

<u>Please Forward</u>

9

REGISTERED

4 inches

14

MS BRENDA J HODGES
4604 COFFMAN LANE
MINNEAPOLIS MN 55406-3644

3

5–6   Joseph G. Jenshak, Jr.
1704 Stewart Avenue
Augusta, GA 30904

2 inches

12

Dr. Lawrence E. Woods
Fair Groves Medical Center
617 Harwick Drive
Augusta, GA 30906

Standard large envelope, No. 10, is 9½ by 4⅛ inches.

Standard small envelope, No. 6¾, is 6½ by 3⅝ inches.

1. RETURN ADDRESS. Business envelopes have a return address printed on the envelope. The writer's name may be typed above the address. On the envelope for a personal letter, the return address begins ½ inch (about 5 or 6 spaces) from the left edge on line 3. Lines are single-spaced and blocked at the left. The personal title *Mr.* should not be used, but other titles may be.

2. ON-ARRIVAL DIRECTIONS. Any on-arrival directions, such as *Personal, Confidential, Please Forward,* or *Hold for Arrival,* should be typed on line 9 and aligned on the left with the return address. These words are typed in capital and lowercase letters and underscored.

3. ADDRESS. Begin the name and address for a small en-velope on line 12, 2 inches (about 20 pica/25 elite spaces) from the left edge; and for a large envelope on line 14, 4 inches (about 40 pica/50 elite spaces) from the left edge. Single-space and block all lines, with the city, state, and ZIP Code on the same line. Type the two-letter abbreviation of the state name, with 1 space before the ZIP Code.

When typing foreign addresses, type the name of the country on a separate final line, in all capitals.

4. SPECIAL MAIL SERVICE. Directions for such mail services as *special delivery, airmail* (overseas only), or *registered* are typed in all-capital letters on line 9. The notation should end ½ inch (about 5 spaces) from the right edge.

ENVELOPE 1 NO. 10 Workguide: 81	From Phyllis A. Cisler. SPECIAL DELIVERY to MR CHARLES R HARRI- SON / RELIABLE SOFTWARE INC / 5613 BRUNSWICK AVENUE NORTH / MINNEAPOLIS MN 55429-2714	10 19 25
ENVELOPE 2 NO. 6¾ Workguide: 83	Confidential from Dr. Carlos P. Decker / 2407 Reed Avenue / Norman, OK 73071. To Ms. Wanda B. Russell / 702 Allenhurst Street / Norman, OK 73071.	11 23 24
ENVELOPE 3 NO. 6¾ Workguide: 83	From J. L. Rogers / Leola Court Apartments, #23 / 3426 Bayou Road / LeBeau, LA 71345. To Mrs. Ellen L. Moreau / 2936 Pineacre Avenue / Davenport, IA 52803.	11 22 26

21-F. SUSTAINED TYPING: SYLLABIC INTENSITY

21-F. Take a 1-minute timing on the first paragraph to establish your base speed. Then take successive 1-minute timings on the other paragraphs. As soon as you equal or exceed your base speed on one paragraph, advance to the next one.

```
26      One should always attempt to maintain good health.  As    12
27  the first step in keeping good health, one should avoid the    24
28  habit of smoking.  Volumes have been written on this topic.    36

29      A second habit that will help maintain your health for    12
30  decades is consuming an appropriate amount of water, day in    24
31  and day out; most physicians recommend eight glasses a day.    36

32      Making exercise a habit is another important trait for    12
33  staying in good health.  Most experts agree that spending a    24
34  few minutes a day in regular, vigorous exercise is helpful.    36

35      A final habit of importance is maintaining appropriate    12
36  body weight.  The key to maintaining weight is developing a    24
37  positive eating pattern.  Calculating calories will assist.    36
    |  |  | 2  | 3  | 4  | 5  | 6  | 7  | 8  | 9  | 10  | 11  | 12
```

21-G. WORD DIVISION

21-G. It is preferable not to divide a word at the end of a line. If it is necessary, however, follow the rules given here.

WP

Many word processors have an automatic hyphenation feature that will (a) automatically divide words too long to fit on one line or (b) highlight those words so that you can insert a hyphen at the appropriate point.

1. Do not divide (a) words pronounced as one syllable (*thoughts, planned*), (b) contractions (*shouldn't, haven't*), or (c) abbreviations (*UNICEF, assoc.*).
2. Divide words only between syllables. Whenever you are unsure of where a syllable ends, consult a dictionary.
3. Leave at least three characters (the last will be a hyphen) on the upper line, and carry at least three characters (the last may be a punctuation mark) to the next line. Thus *de- lay* and *but- ter*, but not *a- maze* or *trick- y*.
4. Divide compound words either at the hyphen (*self- confidence*) or where the two words join to make a solid compound. Thus *master- piece*, not *mas- terpiece*.

21-H. PRODUCTION PRACTICE: WORD DIVISION

21-H. Select the words in each line that can be divided, and type them with a hyphen to show where the division should be (example: *con- sult*).

```
38  rhythm          aren't          going
39  safety          figment         ILGWU
40  grandfather     straight        planned
41  excess          because         couldn't
42  nation          mailbox         stressed
43  children        AMVETS          leading
```

21-I. CENTERING PRACTICE

21-I. Center a double-spaced copy on a half sheet of paper. Spread-center the heading, and block-center the body.

```
         S P R I N G   V A C A T I O N
Daytona Beach, Florida
March 24-31
Leave from STUDENT CENTER
Reasonable Cost for Food, Lodging, and Travel
Call DEBBIE at 555-3244
```

Line: 60 spaces
Tab: 5
Spacing: single
Drills: 2 times
Workguide: 81–86
Format Guide: 33–36
Tape: 23A

LESSON
44

FORMATTING ENVELOPES AND FOLDING LETTERS

Goals: To improve symbol-typing skills; to type 37 wam/3'/5e; to format large and small envelopes; to fold letters for large and small envelopes.

44-A. WARMUP

S 1 A right turn may take them down the road by the clear lake.
A 2 Max questioned Peg Clay as to which five frozen jars broke.
N 3 He saw 26 goats, 57 pigs, 38 cows, 19 horses, and 40 ducks.

SKILLBUILDING

44-B. DIAGNOSTIC TYPING: ALPHABET

Turn to the Diagnostic Typing: Alphabet routine at the back of the book. Take the Pretest, and record your performance on Workguide page 5. Then practice the drill lines for those reaches on which you made errors.

44-C. SYMBOL TYPING

4 The Study Guide* sold @ $9 <u>less</u> a 10% "cash discount."
5 It's likely that Patty and/or her next-door neighbor (Jaime
6 Egan) will do well and get jobs at Kuhn & Mohr at #738 Elm.
7 Gaines & Maxton* sold 7 sets @ $450, a 33 1/3% markup.
8 Janis Roberts (their <u>top</u> salesperson) hasn't sold any #268s
9 yet, but she is "gunning" for the year-end trip to Florida.

44-D. Spacing: double. Record your score.

44-D. SKILL MEASUREMENT: 3-MINUTE TIMED WRITING

10 To be loyal does have different meanings. We might be   12
11 thinking of the trait as it is applied to family members or   24
12 friends. We would all agree that it is used as a patriotic   36
13 word.   37
14 A third use is one with which beginning workers should   49
15 become acquainted. Loyalty to your job and the company for   61
16 which you work is extremely important. You should show you   73
17 care.   74
18 Some of those with whom you work may like to criticize   86
19 the boss or the company in the lounge at every opportunity.   98
20 You, however, can avoid gossip and work for the good of the   110
21 firm.   111

| 1 | 2 | 3 | 4 | 5 | 6 | 7 | 8 | 9 | 10 | 11 | 12 |

Line: 60 spaces
Tab: 5
Spacing: single
Drills: 2 times
Format Guide: 13–14
Tape: 7B or K10B

LESSON 22

SYMBOLS AND WORD DIVISION

Goals: To control the % , ' , and '' keys; to type 28 wam/3'/5e.

22-A. WARMUP

S 1 Todd might fish in the big lake when he visits that island.
A 2 Jack quietly moved up front and seized the big ball of wax.
N 3 He went to Rome on May 30, 1975, and left on July 24, 1986.

22-B. PRACTICE THE KEY

PERCENT is the shift of 5. Use the F finger.

4 ftf ft5f f5f f5%f f5%f f%%f f%%f 5% 55% 78% 52.5% 67.5% f%f
5 Saul was quoted rates of 8%, 9%, 11%, and 13% on the loans.
6 Ramos scored 93% on the test, Sue had 88%, and Al made 84%.

22-C. PRACTICE THE ' KEY

APOSTROPHE is to the right of the semicolon. Use the Sem finger.

7 ;'; ''' ;'; ''' Can't we go on Sue's boat and Chad's plane?
8 Pat's hat, Paul's gloves, and Steve's scarf were all taken.
9 It's Lynn's job to cover Maria's telephone when she's gone.

22-D. PRACTICE THE '' KEY

QUOTATION is the shift of the apostrophe. Use the Sem finger.

10 ;'; '"' ;"; '"' "Super," she said. "That was a super job."
11 The theme of next week's meeting is "Stress in the Office."
12 I watched "Meet the Mets" and "Yankee Power" on the screen.

22-E. Study these rules before typing lines 13–17.

22-E. PLACEMENT OF QUOTATION MARKS

Remember these rules about the placement of quotation marks:
1. The closing quotation mark is always typed *after* a period or comma but *before* a colon or semicolon.
2. The closing quotation mark is typed *after* a question mark or exclamation point if the quoted material is a question or an exclamation; otherwise, the quotation mark is typed *before* the question mark or exclamation point.

13 "Hello," she said. "My name is Stephanie; I'm from Miami."
14 Sara read the article from the text, "Can She Succeed Now?"
15 You said, "I'll mail the check"; however, you didn't do it.
16 Did Jane end the meeting by saying, "We may hit our quota"?
17 Please mark the following items "Important": G361 and F75.

SKILLBUILDING

22-F. NUMBER TYPING

18 She called us at 555-5873 with the 6 orders on September 7.
19 Read Chapters 7, 8, 9, and 10 on pages 60, 75, 85, and 100.
20 On May 28 we will expect to hear from 47 boys and 68 girls.
21 There were 395 votes for Tom, 649 for Sue, and 758 for Pat.

MARGINS. ½ inch on each side. Start the date on line 3 at center.

CLOSING. At center. Leave room for a signature if required; otherwise, leave 1 blank line. The complimentary closing is generally omitted.

REFERENCE INITIALS. Your own.

CARD SIZE. Postcards are 5½ by 3½ inches.

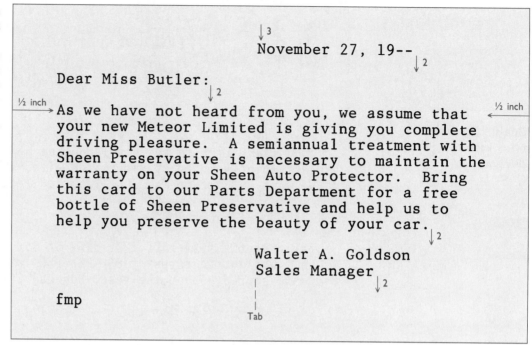

↓3
November 27, 19--
↓2

Dear Miss Butler:
↓2

½ inch → As we have not heard from you, we assume that your new Meteor Limited is giving you complete driving pleasure. A semiannual treatment with Sheen Preservative is necessary to maintain the warranty on your Sheen Auto Protector. Bring this card to our Parts Department for a free bottle of Sheen Preservative and help us to help you preserve the beauty of your car. ½ inch ←
↓2

Walter A. Goldson
Sales Manager
↓2

fmp

Tab

Message Side of Card

POSTCARD 2
Paper: Workguide 77–78

Send the message in Postcard 1 above from Mr. Goldson to Mr. Robert F. Keeley / 38 Overview Court / St. Louis, MO 63128. Use the current date and an appropriate salutation.

POSTCARD 3
Paper: Workguide 79–80

Type a postcard with the following message from Mr. Goldson to Mrs. Joylynn Weston / 3416 Millett Street / East St. Louis, IL 62201.

It was a pleasure for me to meet you when you stopped at our showroom   21
last evening. When I told Jim Burns that you had stopped in, he was truly   36
disappointed that he was not here to see you. I told him that you were   51
considering the purchase of a new car, so he may have called you by the   64
time this card arrives. As our inventory is at an all-time high, Jim will be   79
able to help you find just the car you want.   96

POSTCARD 4
Paper: Workguide 79–80

The last postcard contains the following message from Mr. Goldson to Mr. William J. Arthur / 8725 Bremerton Road / St. Louis, MO 63144.

Dear Bill: We at Dobson are as pleased as you are that the convertible   18
you bought last year has not given you any problems. You should be   32
aware, however, that the original one-year warranty expires on the first   46
of next month. Consequently, we recommend that you consider pur-   59
chasing an extended coverage policy for continued protection. I shall   73
look forward to your call at 555-3864; or if convenient, please stop in for   88
a cup of coffee.   98

22-G. CONCENTRATION PRACTICE

22-G. Spell out all numbers as you type lines 22–25. All lines will end evenly.

22 There were 4 girls and 7 boys at the birthday party.
23 We saw 2 movies, 4 concerts, and 5 plays last week.
24 She wants 2 more workers, 9 altogether, here at 7.
25 The 2 girls won 1st and 3rd place in the 6th event.

22-H. 12-SECOND SPRINTS

22-H. Take three 12-second timings on each line. The scale gives your wam speed for each 12-second timing. (If you cannot be timed, type each line twice.)

26 Plan to join our team at the mall when you finish your job.
27 When it is time to work, be sure that you do the very best.
28 Find a quiet place when it is time to do all your homework.
29 The trip being planned for this weekend should be pleasant.

    5   10   15   20   25   30   35   40   45   50   55   60

22-I. PACED PRACTICE

Turn to the Paced Practice routine at the back of the book. Take several 2-minute timings, starting at the point where you left off the last time. Record your progress on Workguide page 6.

22-J. SKILL MEASUREMENT: 3-MINUTE TIMED WRITING

22-J. Spacing: double. Record your score.

30   Jobs in business require good communication skills for   12
31 success. Confirmation of this fact can be found in various   24
32 magazines and books.   28
33   It is expected that a new worker in business will have   40
34 the ability to speak and write clearly and properly. These   52
35 are critical skills.   56
36   While there are many attributes needed for success, it   68
37 should be obvious that having good communication skills can   80
38 be a gigantic asset.   84

    | | | 2 | 3 | 4 | 5 | 6 | 7 | 8 | 9 | 10 | 11 | 12

22-K. PRODUCTION PRACTICE: WORD DIVISION

22-K. Select the words that can be divided, and type them with a hyphen to show where the division should be (example: under- stand).

39	understand	USSR	maintain
40	along	thoughts	wasn't
41	abundant	staged	varsity
42	person	self-evident	planned
43	isn't	mailable	awake
44	NABTE	section	design
45	weighed	transmit	o'clock
46	withhold	breach	service
47	through	shouldn't	senator-elect

POSTCARDS

Line: 60 spaces
Spacing: single
Drills: 2 times
Workguide: 77–80
Format Guide: 33–34
Tape: 23A

Goals: To improve speed and accuracy; to improve proofreading skills; to format postcards.

43-A. WARMUP

S 1 Mel and Pam may take a bus to visit their aunt in late May.
A 2 Geoffrey Braxmont quickly drove past the wild jazz concert.
N 3 There were 1,602 students compared with 534 in August 1987.

SKILLBUILDING

43-B. Retype this announcement, correcting errors as you type.

43-B. PRODUCTION PRACTICE: PROOFREADING

4 A new service weill be provided for all employes of Dobson,
5 Inc beginnning on january 1, 19--. The new Human Resources
6 Department will initiate a series of worksshops onthe topic
7 of "Personal Financial planning". After covering the topic
8 of budjets, we well give attention to such things as these:
9 how to save, bying, a house, taxes, investments, retirement
10 planing, wills, estate planing, and subjects of interest...

43-C. FORMATTING A POSTCARD

Study the illustration and notations below and in the left margin; then, using the postcard forms on Workguide pages 77–80, type Postcards 1–4.

POSTCARD 1

Line: 45 pica/55 elite spaces
Tab: 2 inches, center
Spacing: single
Paper: Workguide 77–78

RETURN ADDRESS. Blocked on line 3, ½ inch from left edge. The personal title *Mr.* should not be used, but other titles such as *Dr.* or *Mrs.* may be used.
ADDRESS. Blocked on line 12, 2 inches from left edge.

Note: Single-space all addresses. Type the city, state, and ZIP Code on one line; leave 1 space between the state abbreviation and the ZIP Code.

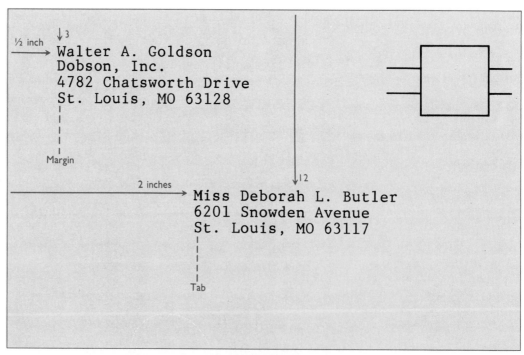

Address Side of Card

SYMBOLS AND LINE-ENDING DECISIONS

Line: 60 spaces
Tab: 5
Spacing: single
Drills: 2 times
Workguide: 33–34
Format Guide: 13–14
Tape: 8B or K11B

Goals: To control the &, $, and _ keys; to make correct line-ending decisions; to improve speed and accuracy.

23-A. WARMUP

S 1 If the work is done correctly, the group may make a profit.
A 2 Working quietly, Max alphabetized the census of vital jobs.
N 3 Our store will be open from 7:30 to 9:45 on December 18-26.

23-B. PRACTICE THE & KEY

&
7

AMPERSAND (sign for *and*) is the shift of 7. Use the J finger.

4 juj ju7j j7j j7&j j&&j j&&j Max & Di & Sue & Tom & Vi & Kay
5 The case of Ball & Trup vs. Crane & Vens will start May 10.
6 Rudd & Sons bought their ten tickets from Cross & Thompson.

23-C. PRACTICE THE $ KEY

$
4

DOLLAR is the shift of 4. Use the F finger.

7 frf fr4f f4f f4$f f$$f f$$f $44, $444, $4,444, $44.40, $440
8 She received quotes of $48, $52, and $76 for the old radio.
9 Our insurance paid $625 for the accident; I paid only $150.

23-D. PRACTICE THE _ KEY

_

UNDERSCORE is the shift of the hyphen. Use the Sem finger.

Note: Underscore individual words separately; for a book title, underscore the entire title, including the spaces.

10 ;p; ;p-; ;-; ;-_; ;__; ;__; wouldn't or couldn't; me or we;
11 Rebecca should use The American Heritage School Dictionary.
12 Be sure that you used the words to, too, and two correctly.

23-F. Select and insert *you, your,* or *you're* in place of each dash.

SKILLBUILDING

23-E. TECHNIQUE TYPING: SHIFT/CAPS LOCK

13 MR. ANGELO P. ANGELOZZI of 241 Fifth Avenue was the winner.
14 Will they be going to SAN DIEGO or to PITTSBURGH next week?
15 The important GAME pits EAST CHESTNUT HIGH vs. BATTON HIGH.
16 Our BETA SIGMA chapter will attend the meeting in PORTLAND.

23-F. CONCENTRATION PRACTICE

17 -- should buy -- three tickets to the show by next week.
18 -- quite correct when -- note that -- bill is wrong.
19 -- correct in noting that -- thoughts make -- happy.
20 -- should balance -- checkbook with -- bank statement.

42-E. MEMORANDUMS

Type the memorandums below, using the same formatting procedures that were used for the memorandums on page 83. Work to improve your speed as you quickly move through the *MEMO TO, FROM, DATE,* and *SUBJECT* lines.

MEMO 3

Paper: plain, half sheet

MEMO TO: Elmer Foster, General Manager / FROM: Elizabeth Blom- 13
quist, Computer Operations / DATE: November 18, 19— / SUBJECT: 25
Implementation of Word Processing Center 33

    I have compiled the data you requested regarding the need for a word 47
processing center for our central offices. There are many advantages to 62
the implementation of such a system. During the past month, informa- 75
tion has been gathered from various departments regarding their antici- 89
pated use of the center. 94

    As we agreed in our telephone conversation earlier this morning, I will 108
send you a comprehensive report of my findings in the next few days. 122
We will then meet to discuss the report on November 26. / *(Your* 133
initials) 134

MEMO 4

Paper: plain, full sheet

WP
    Many word processors have a rapid form-fill-in feature that automatically prints each line of the heading for a memo, pausing to allow the operator to key in the variable information on each line.

An attachment notation is used if the material mentioned is to be physically attached to the memorandum. An enclosure notation is used if the material is enclosed in the same envelope with the memorandum. Type either notation at the left margin, a single space below the reference initials.

MEMO TO: Elmer Foster 4
                General Manager 7
FROM: Elizabeth Bloomquist 13
                Computer Operations 17
DATE: November 22, 19-- 22
SUBJECT: Implementation of Word Processing Center 32

In my memo of November 18 [17], I said that I would forward my 44
recommendations for the implementation of a word processing 56
center at our central offices. A detailed report is attached. 68

Our current level of secretarial support appears to be inade- 80
quate. There are often delays of from four to seven days. 92

There micro computers with word#processing software will be 104
made available to the computer center. We think that delays 116
can be held to two days by retraining present employees. I 128
will expand on these recomendations at our meeting on november 140
26. 141

pck 142

Attachment 144

23-G. Take two 1-minute timings. Note that the last two digits of each number provide a cumulative word count to help you determine your speed.

23-G. NUMBER TYPING

21	4701	3802	2903	1004	5605	7406	8307	9208	6509	4710	3811	2912
22	1013	5614	7415	8316	9217	6518	4719	3820	2921	1022	5623	7424
23	8325	9226	6527	4728	3829	2930	1031	5632	7433	8334	9235	6536
24	4737	3838	2939	1040	5641	7442	8343	9244	6545	4746	3847	2948

23-H. Not all typewriters are alike, so check yours to see how many spaces are left after the warning bell rings and before the keys lock at the right margin.

WP Computers and word processors have an automatic carrier return called *word wrap* that advances to the next line as each line becomes full. The automatic word wrap eliminates the need for a manual return at the end of a line.

23-H. MAKING LINE-ENDING DECISIONS

When you cannot type material line for line, you must decide where each line should end. To help you end lines *without looking up,* a bell rings when the carrier is 8 to 10 spaces from the right margin. For example, if you wish lines to end at 75 and have therefore set the margin at 80, the bell may ring when the carrier reaches 70—signaling that you have 10 spaces left before the keys lock at the margin, and only 5 spaces left before you reach the *desired* ending point of 75. When the bell rings, end the line as near to the *desired* line ending as possible (preferably without dividing a word).

For example, if your typewriter gives an 8-space warning, here are some typical line-ending decisions you might encounter:

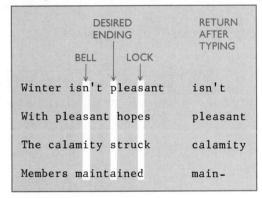

23-I. PRODUCTION PRACTICE: LINE-ENDING DECISIONS

The timed writing in 22-J on page 40 is shown on a 60-space line. Set your margins for a 50-space line and type it again. Decide where to end each line. Listen for the bell and *do not look up*. If time permits, repeat the exercise using a 70-space line.

23-J. Center the exercise on a half sheet of paper. Spread-center the title, and block-center the notice.

23-J. CENTERING PRACTICE

N O T I C E ↓3

The Affirmative Action Committee will be meeting on Thursday, October 18, in Room C-310. The meeting will be chaired by Connie Walters, director. The following items will be discussed: ↓2

1. Current Profile of Support Personnel
2. Current Profile of Professional Staff
3. Revision of Reporting Forms
4. Change in Interviewing Form
5. Goal for Hiring of Support Personnel
6. Goal for Hiring of Professional Staff

MEMORANDUMS

Line: 60 spaces
Tab: 5
Spacing: single
Drills: 2 times
Format Guide: 31–32
Tape: 22A

Goals: To type 36 wam/3'/5e; to improve skills in typing punctuation marks; to format interoffice memorandums.

42-A. WARMUP

S 1 Henry got six tickets to the game for half the usual price.
A 2 Dave and Peggy quickly mixed the frozen berries with juice.
N 3 The three doctors delivered 305 girls and 264 boys in 1987.

SKILLBUILDING

42-B. SUSTAINED TYPING: PUNCTUATION

42-B. Take a 1-minute timing on the first paragraph to establish your base speed. Then take several 1-minute timings on the remaining paragraphs. As soon as you equal or exceed your base speed on one paragraph, advance to the next one.

4   Changes in federal tax laws in recent years have had a   12
5 real effect on the paychecks of office workers. The social   24
6 security tax rate went up while income tax rates went down.   36

7   However, the result has been modest increases in take-   12
8 home pay for most people. Some workers are now looking for   24
9 places to invest; they want their savings to work for them.   36

10   Safety must be the <u>small</u> investor's main concern; rate   12
11 of return and availability are secondary. Will those sure-   24
12 fire, unbeatable schemes lead you to think any differently?   36

13   Those investments (savings) won't make one rich, but a   12
14 regular investment plan <u>will help</u> to "ease one into retire-   24
15 ment." A first-rate rule is: Watch for a tempter's snare.   36

   | | | 2 | 3 | 4 | 5 | 6 | 7 | 8 | 9 | 10 | 11 | 12

42-C. PACED PRACTICE

Turn to the Paced Practice routine at the back of the book. Take several 2-minute timings, starting at the speed at which you left off the last time. Record your progress on Workguide page 6.

42-D. Spacing: double. Record your score.

42-D. SKILL MEASUREMENT: 3-MINUTE TIMED WRITING

16   We must not make the mistake of thinking that computer   12
17 technology is limited to the office. A stop at a fast-food   24
18 place recently forced me to think about this for some time.   36
19   My friend and I quickly gave our orders to a young man   48
20 at the counter. The young man keyed in codes for each item   60
21 and then turned to the next one in line. We could see five   72
22 cooks through an opening that I would judge to be four feet   84
23 by six feet in size. One of the cooks read our orders on a   96
24 kitchen monitor; our bill was being automatically computed. 108

   | | | 2 | 3 | 4 | 5 | 6 | 7 | 8 | 9 | 10 | 11 | 12

SYMBOLS AND ERROR CORRECTION

Line: 60 spaces
Tab: 5
Spacing: single
Drills: 2 times
Format Guide: 13–14
Tape: 9B or K12B

Goals: To control the @ and * keys; to learn different error-correction processes; to type 29 wam/3'/5e.

AT is the shift of 2. Use the S finger.

ASTERISK is the shift of 8. Use the K finger.

24-A. WARMUP

S 1 The downtown firms that produce maps of islands have moved.
A 2 The day her film took a prize box, Jacqueline was vigorous.
N 3 With 37,548 fans screaming, we won the game 10-9 on May 26.

24-B. PRACTICE THE @ KEY

4 sws sw2s s2s s2@s s2@s s@@s s@@s Buy 15 @ $44 and 18 @ $55.
5 We will sell him 14 units @ $9, 8 units @ $15, and 5 @ $21.
6 Order 12 items @ $114, 9 @ $99, and another 18 items @ $87.

24-C. PRACTICE THE * KEY

7 kik ki8k k8k k8*k k8*k k**k k**k *** Tom's article* is new.
8 The * sign, the asterisk, is used for reference purposes.**
9 The asterisk symbol, ***, is ideal for typing a border. ***

SKILLBUILDING

PRETEST. Take a 1-minute timing; compute your speed and count errors.

24-D. PRETEST: COMMON LETTER COMBINATIONS

10   The manager tried to react with total control. He was   12
11 indeed annoyed and devoted all his efforts to being fair to   24
12 the entire staff. His daily schedule was rampant with ways   36
13 in which to confront the situation and to apply good sense.   48
 | | | 2 | 3 | 4 | 5 | 6 | 7 | 8 | 9 | 10 | 11 | 12

PRACTICE.
   Speed Emphasis: If you made 2 or fewer errors on the Pretest, type each line twice.
   Accuracy Emphasis: If you made 3 or more errors, type each group of lines (e.g., 14–17) as though it were a paragraph, twice.

24-E. PRACTICE: WORD BEGINNINGS

14 re relay react reply reuse reason record return results red
15 in index inept incur inset inning indeed insure interns ink
16 be beast berry being beeps berate belong became beavers bet
17 de dealt death decay devil detest devote derive depicts den

24-F. PRACTICE: WORD ENDINGS

18 ly dimly daily apply lowly barely deeply unruly finally sly
19 ed cured moved tamed tried amused billed busted creamed fed
20 nt mount blunt front stunt absent rodent splint rampant ant
21 al canal total local equal plural rental verbal logical pal

POSTTEST. Repeat the Pretest and compare performance.

24-G. POSTTEST: COMMON LETTER COMBINATIONS

24-H. ERROR CORRECTION

An error should be corrected as soon as it is made. Since you may not know when you make an error, however, always be sure to proofread your work carefully and

MEMO 1

Line: 6 inches (60 pica/70 elite)
Tab: 10
Paper: plain, half sheet

↓7   Tab

MEMO TO: Shirley DeWitt, Accounting Department   9
                                                      ↓2
FROM: Michael Andresen, Manager   16
                                                ↓2
DATE: November 10, 19--   22
                                            ↓2
SUBJECT: Meeting on Computer Networking   30
                                                  ↓3

This will confirm this morning's telephone conversation in   42
which I indicated that I would like to meet with all depart- 53
ment heads in our Finance Division concerning the implementa- 65
tion of computer networking.   71
                             ↓2
The meeting will begin at 9 a.m. on November 21 and will be   83
held in the conference room on the sixth floor. Peter Frank, 94
vice president for information services, will address the   106
group and will be available for questions.   115
                                            ↓2
kae   116

MEMO 2

Line: 6 inches (60 pica/70 elite)
Tab: 10
Paper: Workguide 75

WP   Some word pro-
cessors enable the user to
program margins and tab
stops that will then be saved
for future use. Others store
the heading lines so that
only variable text has to be
keyed in.

↓13   Tab

MEMO TO: Earl L. Schlee, Senior Vice President   7
                                                      ↓2
FROM: Michael Andresen, Manager   12
                                                ↓2
DATE: November 22, 19—   16
                                            ↓2
SUBJECT: Computer Networking in Finance Division   24
                                                      ↓3

Computer networking in the Finance Division was discussed at a meet- 37
ing on November 21, and the staff was very receptive to the ideas pre- 51
sented.   52
        ↓2
Peter Frank, vice president for information services, addressed the   66
group on the advantages and disadvantages of networking. He also out- 80
lined a five-phase plan to integrate networking into our present system. 94
Following the presentation, a number of questions and ideas were dis- 108
cussed.   109
        ↓2
Specific departmental applications will be addressed at our next meeting 124
early in December.   128
                  ↓2
kae   129

correct any errors that you find *before* removing the paper from the typewriter or before storing a document on a word processor. Correcting errors while the paper is still in the machine is much easier than having to reinsert the paper and align the type. Also, correcting an error on a computer before a document is stored saves the time of recalling the document and making the correction.

Use one of the following techniques to correct errors:

Correction Ribbon. Typewriters with correction capabilities contain a correction ribbon as well as a special backspace key that engages the correction ribbon. (1) Use the special backspace key to backspace to the error. (2) Retype the error so that the coating on the correction ribbon lifts the error off the typing page. (3) Type the correction.

Backspace/Strikeover. To correct an error on electronic typewriters, word processors, or computers: (1) Depress the backspace key or correction key to erase the incorrect characters. (2) Type the correct characters. The correct characters replace the incorrect ones. This method may vary according to the equipment used.

Correction Paper. Slips of paper that contain a light coating of chalk can also be used to correct an error. (1) Backspace to the error and place the correction paper between the typing paper and the typewriter ribbon (coated side toward the typing paper). (2) Retype the error. (The chalk from the correction paper will conceal the error.) (3) Remove the correction paper, backspace, and type the correction.

Correction Fluid. Correction fluid works similarly to correction paper in that it covers the error. (1) Turn the paper forward or backward. (2) Brush the fluid sparingly over the error. (3) Let the fluid dry. (4) Type the correction.

Typing Eraser. (1) Lift the paper bail and turn the platen to move the error into position for easy access. (2) To keep eraser crumbs from falling into the mechanism, move the carrier to the extreme left or right—away from the error. (3) Use a stiff ink eraser and a *light* up-and-down motion to erase the error. (4) Return to the typing line and type the correction.

24-I. Type lines 22–25; then make the following corrections:
Lines 22 and 23: Change *Kim* to *Jim*.
Lines 24 and 25: Change *four* to *five*.

24-I. PRODUCTION PRACTICE: ERROR CORRECTION

22 Kim's brother showed Kim how to fix the damaged automobile.
23 When Kim went to Sue's house, Kim found the old photograph.
24 The four students took twelve trips in the past four years.
25 Four errors are usually allowed in timings of four minutes.

SKILLBUILDING

24-J. Spacing: double. Record your score.

24-J. SKILL MEASUREMENT: 3-MINUTE TIMED WRITING

26 Airports can be interesting places to visit. Being in 12
27 a crowded airport lobby will make one realize just how much 24
28 our society is on the move. 29
29 The number of people who fly on any given day is quite 41
30 high. Experts say the number of passengers will get higher 53
31 in the next several years. 58
32 As the number of flights increases at many airports, a 70
33 good number of flights are delayed in departing. Officials 82
34 hope to solve the problem. 87

| 1 | 2 | 3 | 4 | 5 | 6 | 7 | 8 | 9 | 10 | 11 | 12 |

LESSON
41

MEMORANDUMS

Line: 60 spaces
Tab: 5
Spacing: single
Drills: 2 times
Workguide: 75
Format Guide: 31–32
Tape: 21A

Goals: To improve speed and accuracy; to format interoffice memorandums.

41-A. WARMUP

S 1 She may make eight right angles when she works on the maps.
A 2 Sixty-five amazed children kept quiet with our big justice.
N 3 They won the three games by 46 to 20, 35 to 9, and 17 to 8.

SKILLBUILDING

PRETEST. Take a 1-minute timing; compute your speed and count errors.

41-B. PRETEST: DISCRIMINATION PRACTICE

4   Few of you were as lucky as Bev was when she joined us   12
5 for golf. She just dreaded the looks of the work crew when   24
6 she goofed. But she neatly swung a club and aced the hole.   36
   | 1 | 2 | 3 | 4 | 5 | 6 | 7 | 8 | 9 | 10 | 11 | 12

PRACTICE.
   Speed Emphasis: If you made 2 or fewer errors on the Pretest, type each line twice.
   Accuracy Emphasis: If you made 3 or more errors, type each group of lines as though it were a paragraph, twice.

41-C. PRACTICE: LEFT HAND

7 vbv verb bevy vibes bevel brave above verbal bovine behaves
8 wew west weep threw wedge weave fewer weight sewing dewdrop
9 ded deed seed bride guide dealt cried secede parted precede
10 fgf gulf gift fight fudge fugue flags flight golfer feigned

41-D. PRACTICE: RIGHT HAND

11 klk kiln lake knoll lanky locks liken kettle kindle knuckle
12 uyu buys your usury unity youth buoys unruly untidy younger
13 oio coin lion oiled foils foist prior oilcan iodine iodized
14 jhj jury huge enjoy three judge habit adjust slight jasmine

POSTTEST. Repeat the Pretest and compare performance.

41-E. POSTTEST: DISCRIMINATION PRACTICE

41-F. DIAGNOSTIC TYPING: NUMBERS

Turn to the Diagnostic Typing: Numbers routine at the back of the book. Take the Pretest, and record your performance on Workguide page 5. Then practice the drill lines for those reaches on which you made errors.

41-G. FORMATTING AN INTEROFFICE MEMORANDUM

An interoffice memorandum is a message from one person to another in the same organization. It may be typed on plain paper, on a special memorandum form, or on letterhead stationery, using either a half sheet or a full sheet of paper. Follow these steps in typing a memorandum on either plain paper or letterhead stationery:

1. Use a 6-inch line (60 pica/70 elite).
2. Begin typing the heading on line 7 on half sheets of paper and on line 13 on full sheets of paper.
3. Set a 10-space tab to align the heading information.
4. Leave 2 blank lines before the body of the memorandum.
5. Include your reference initials. (The writer's initials are optional.)

Line: 60 spaces
Tab: 5
Spacing: single
Drills: 2 times
Format Guide: 13–16
Tape: 10B or K12B

Goals: To control optional symbols; to construct special symbols; to improve speed and accuracy.

25-A. WARMUP

S 1 Half of the corn in that big field may be cut by six hands.
A 2 Jack quietly gave some of his prize boxes to the dog owner.
N 3 The 29 teachers and 754 students arrived at 8:30 on May 16.

25-B. Take 1-minute timings on each paragraph. Then take a 2-minute timing on both paragraphs together. Stress technique and accuracy rather than speed.

25-B. SYMBOL TYPING

4 Sam said, "Order 33# of the #100 crates." You can try
5 to order them from Smith & Clay (call V & J if needed). If
6 the old price of 1 pound @ $3 holds, the total will be $99.
7 Since our 25% discount was not shown on Invoice #3434,
8 Mr. DeVries will <u>not</u> want to send the check for $543 unless
9 B & W sends a debit memo (or letter) to correct the record.

¢ / 6
CENT is the shift of 6 on some keyboards. Use the J finger.

! / 1
EXCLAMATION is the shift of the 1 on most keyboards. Use the A finger.

+ / =
EQUAL is to the right of the hyphen on most keyboards. Use the sem finger.

+ / =
PLUS is the shift of EQUAL. Use the Sem finger.

25-C. PRACTICE THE ¢, !, =, AND + KEYS

10 jyj jy6j j6j j6¢j j6¢j j¢¢j j¢¢j Alan paid 6¢ and 56¢ each.
11 They spent 10¢, 29¢, 38¢, 47¢, and 56¢ for the new pencils.
12 aqa aq1a a1a a1!a a1!a a!!a a!!a Where! What! Why! When!
13 The blast-off is nearing: Five! Four! Three! Two! One!
14 ;=; ;=; ;==; ;==; ;==; Let A = 50; Let B = 75; Let C = 100!
15 If B = 10, then 60; if B = 20, then 70; if B = 30, then 80.
16 ;=; ;=+; ;=+; ;++; ;++; 8 + 8 = 16; 7 + 7 = 14; 6 + 6 = 12.
17 When you add 30 + 40 + 50 + 60 + 70 + 80 + 90, you get 420.

25-D. CONSTRUCTING SPECIAL SYMBOLS

times	18 What is 9 x 6?	Small letter *x*.
minus	19 129 - 73 = 56.	Hyphen.
divided by	20 121 ÷ 11 = 11.	Colon, backspace, hyphen.
feet and inches	21 Rose is 5' 7".	Apostrophe (feet), quotation marks (inches).
fractions	22 8/10 = 80/100.	Numerator, diagonal, denominator.
minutes and seconds	23 10' 45" to go.	Apostrophe (minutes), quotation mark (seconds).
exclamation	24 I will not go!	Period, backspace, apostrophe.
brackets	25 They /‾Indians‾/	Diagonals, with underscores facing inside.

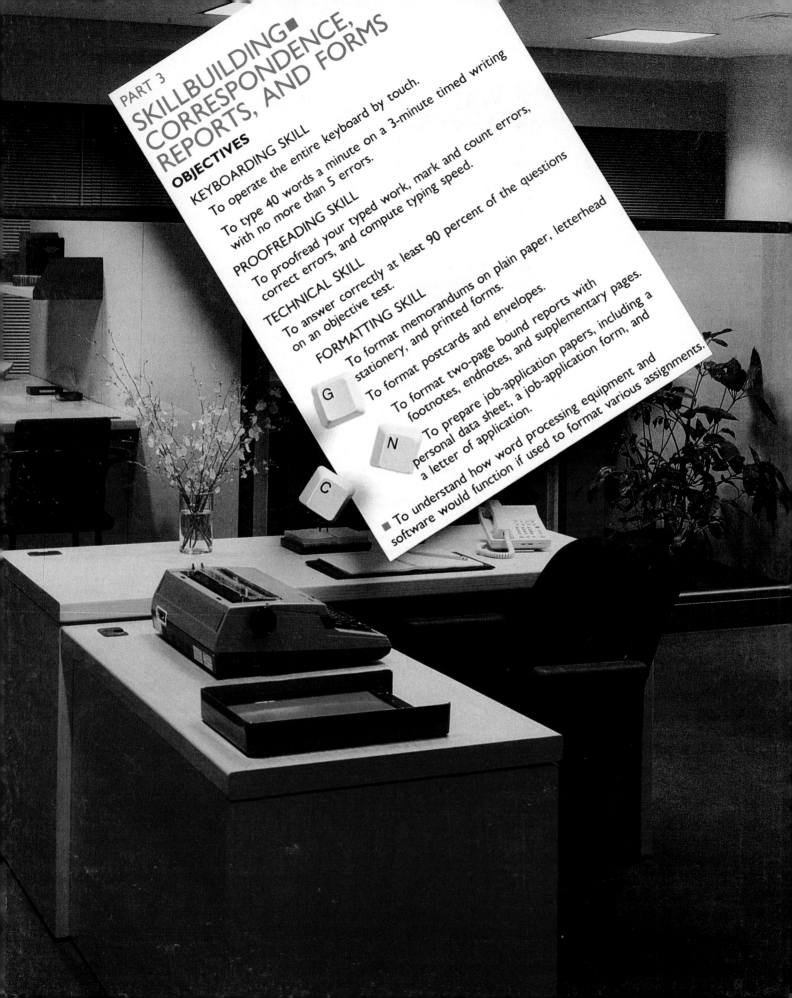

PART 3

SKILLBUILDING■ CORRESPONDENCE, REPORTS, AND FORMS

OBJECTIVES

KEYBOARDING SKILL

To operate the entire keyboard by touch.

To type 40 words a minute on a 3-minute timed writing with no more than 5 errors.

PROOFREADING SKILL

To proofread your typed work, mark and count errors, correct errors, and compute typing speed.

TECHNICAL SKILL

To answer correctly at least 90 percent of the questions on an objective test.

FORMATTING SKILL

To format memorandums on plain paper, letterhead stationery, and printed forms.

To format postcards and envelopes.

To format two-page bound reports with footnotes, endnotes, and supplementary pages.

To prepare job-application papers, including a personal data sheet, a job-application form, and a letter of application.

■ To understand how word processing equipment and software would function if used to format various assignments.

25-E. Set tabs every 15 spaces. Use the tab key to go from column to column.

25-E. TECHNIQUE TYPING: TAB KEY

26 Being   productive   at   information
27 processing   will   be   enhanced
28 by   having   individuals   who
29 know   how   to   keyboard.

25-F. Type each sentence on a separate line.

25-F. TECHNIQUE TYPING: RETURN/ENTER KEY

30 Where are they going? Who is going? When will you return?
31 The hat was red. The scarf was pink. The gloves were tan.
32 Joe sang. Stu read. Ro walked. Vin cried. Pat screamed.
33 What score did you get on the test? Was it an improvement?

25-G. PRODUCTION PRACTICE: LINE-ENDING DECISIONS

The skill measurement timed writing in 24-J on page 44 is shown on a 60-space line. Set your margins for a 70-space line, and type the three paragraphs. Decide for yourself where to end each line. Listen for the bell and *do not look up.* If time permits, repeat this exercise using a 50-space line.

25-H. Take a 1-minute timing on the first paragraph to establish your base speed. Then take successive 1-minute timings on the other paragraphs. As soon as you equal or exceed your base speed on one paragraph, advance to the next one.

25-H. SUSTAINED TYPING: NUMBERS AND SYMBOLS

34   Our sales to Johnson & Clark showed an increase of 30%   12
35 over the same month last year. Last year we sold them $650   24
36 worth of merchandise in May; sales for this year were $845.   36

37   Shipment of items on Invoice #478 (radios, tape decks,   12
38 & stereos) was to be postponed to June 12. The delay would   24
39 mean that our cash flow for May would be reduced by $3,605.   36

40   Errors were found on these invoices: (#336, #391, and   12
41 #402). The errors resulted in a shortfall of revenue. For   24
42 the year, errors have gone up 22%. This must be corrected!   36

   | 1 | 2 | 3 | 4 | 5 | 6 | 7 | 8 | 9 | 10 | 11 | 12

25-I. Take three 12-second timings on each line. The scale gives your wam speed for each 12-second timing.

25-I. 12-SECOND SPRINTS

X 43 Max took the sixty extra index cards from the box for Alex.
J 44 Jack, John, and Jacob just enjoyed the juice from Al's jug.
Q 45 That unique equation on the quiz made Quentin quit quickly.
Z 46 Zeke was amazed at the prize that Lizzy won at that bazaar.

       5   10   15   20   25   30   35   40   45   50   55   60

25-J. Center a double-spaced copy on a half sheet of paper. Spread-center the title, and block-center the body.

25-J. CENTERING PRACTICE

                       P B L   W I N N E R S
        Transcription: Eileen Murray
        Public Speaking: Susan Angelozzi
        Future Teacher: Stanley Barusiwicz
        Typewriting: Stephen White
        Shorthand: Mary Rubino
        Business Math: Elaine Gallo

TEST 2-C
TABLE 12

Spacing: double
Paper: Workguide 71

Center horizontally and vertically.

REPRODATA EQUIPMENT, INC. 5

Copier Sales for October 10

Model	Number	Percent	
			13
Paramount D2000	347	35.1	18
Zenith C4000	210	21.2	22
Embassy 21XL50	148	14.9	26
Zenith C3051	121	12.2	30
Paramount D1200	89	9.0	34
Embassy 40XX20	57	5.8	37
Paramount D4000	18	1.8	41

TEST 2-D
REPORT 11

Spacing: double
Paper: Workguide 73

NEW PHONE SERVICES 4

By Gail Okun 6

Telephone service has become quiet sophisticated in the 17
past few years. Call forwarding, call waiting, and speed call 30
service are already available to ~~some~~ many customers. Two new 41
services will soon be available to ~~many~~ some private and business 54
clients: return call and call screening. 62

RETURN CALL 64

This service will ~~enable~~ allow a customer to return the most 75
recent incoming call, even it it was not answered. This 86
feature will help to call back that person who might call ~~you~~ 98
at an inopportune time when you can't answer the telphone. 110

Call Screening 112

Screening calls can be extremely beneficial to any 123
customer. Two services are call block and call trace. 133

Call Block. This feature will give the ~~client~~ customer the 144
ability to stop all calls originating from specific tele- 155
phone numbers. The caller hears a ring, but the ~~client~~ customer does 168
not. This means that one can chose not to talk [to selected individuals]. 182

Call Trace. This service will ~~allow~~ enable a customer to 193
initiate an automatic trace of the last call recieved. This 205
can assist one who is receiving [anonymous] calls of any type. 217

LESSON
26

Line: 60 spaces
Tab: 5
Spacing: single
Drills: 2 times
Workguide: 35–41
Format Guide: 15–16
Tape: 11B

LETTER TYPING

Goals: To type 30 wam/3'/5e; to format a business letter.

26-A. WARMUP

S 1 They paid the four men to handle the forty bushels of corn.
A 2 Jay gave an expert a quick breakdown of all the sizes made.
N 3 Call 555-3190 and clarify our $826.47 charge for equipment.

SKILLBUILDING

26-B. Type lines 4–7 twice each. In these We-23 drills, each number uses the same reaches as the preceding word.

26-B. NUMBER TYPING

4 we 23 et 35 ore 943 tie 483 rot 495 toy 596 the 563 you 697
5 up 70 re 43 pie 083 ire 843 top 590 yet 635 owe 923 owl 929
6 it 85 or 94 yet 635 pup 070 wit 285 pit 085 out 975 rip 480
7 to 59 ie 83 pet 035 yet 635 two 529 tip 580 wet 235 put 075

26-C. Type line 8. Then type lines 9–11 reading the words from right to left.

26-C. CONCENTRATION PRACTICE

8 When keyboarding, always strive for complete concentration.
9 concentration. complete for strive always keyboarding, When
10 left. to right from sentence the typing by up looking Avoid
11 words. over skips often copy the from up looks who typist A

26-D. Compare this paragraph with the second paragraph of the letter on page 49. Type a list of the words that contain errors, correcting the errors as you type.

26-D. PRODUCTION PRACTICE: PROOFREADING

12 We would like to invite you to a special sesion, desined to
13 provide more detailed formation about our service, which we
14 are sponsering for people from the Dallas area. The session
15 will be held on Tuesday, March 6, in Raybern Hall of the
16 Dallas Convention center. It will begin at 9 a.m.

26-E. Spacing: double. Record your score.

26-E. SKILL MEASUREMENT: 3-MINUTE TIMED WRITING

17   Time is precious. Whether you are at work or at home, 12
18 you only have a set number of hours at your disposal. Plan 24
19 to use all your time wisely. 30
20   Employers like to see workers who zip along at a quick 42
21 pace. Of course, it is just as important that the work you 54
22 complete be free of mistakes. 60
23   Be sure that you take time for yourself at home. If a 72
24 few extra minutes or hours become available, consider doing 84
25 a special treat for yourself. 90

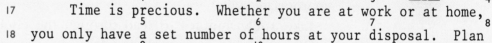

Ask your instructor for the General Information Test on Part 2.

T E S T

PROGRESS TEST ON PART 2

TEST 2-A
3-MINUTE TIMED WRITING

Line: 60 spaces
Tab: 5
Spacing: double
Paper: Workguide 67
Start: 6 lines from top

```
                 1              2              3            4
    Now that you have completed the first forty lessons of    12
         5            6            7            8
this text, let us hope that you are quite pleased with your    24
          9           10           11          12
level of progress thus far.  Learning to type the different    36
       13            14           15          16
keys by touch was followed by attempts to improve the speed    48
       17            18           19          20
and accuracy of your stroking.  You have now completed your    60
      21           22            23          24
first cycle of typing letters, reports, and tables.  If you    72
       25             26           27          28
analyze the next part of the text, you will see a continued    84
        29            30            31          32
push to increase your stroking skill.  There will also be a    96
       33            34            35          36
great deal of emphasis put on increasing production skills.   108
  |   |   | 2 | 3 | 4 | 5 | 6 | 7 | 8 | 9 | 10 | 11 | 12
```

TEST 2-B
LETTER 14
MODIFIED-BLOCK STYLE

Paper: Workguide 69

(Current date) / Ms. Gail Hentz / Vice President for Administration /   13
Oliver Temporary Services / 65 McPherson Street / Danville, KY 40422 /   26
Dear Ms. Hentz: 29

Are you having difficulty finding individuals who possess the skills and   43
training that employers look for in their temporary employees? Could   57
you benefit from having prospective employees who have additional   71
appropriate skills?   74

Take a few minutes to read through the enclosed brochure. It de-   87
scribes a training program that we have developed to help you train your   102
temporary workers in those skills which are in high demand by potential   116
employers.   118

If you wish, we will send you this instructional package on a free,   132
ten-day trial basis. Just use the order slip in the brochure to get your   147
copy. We are confident that once you use this exciting new program,   160
you will be able to increase your rate of placement of temporary   173
workers.   174

Sincerely yours, / Donald C. Williams / Account Executive / *(Your*   184
initials) / Enclosure   187

26-F. BASIC PARTS OF A BUSINESS LETTER

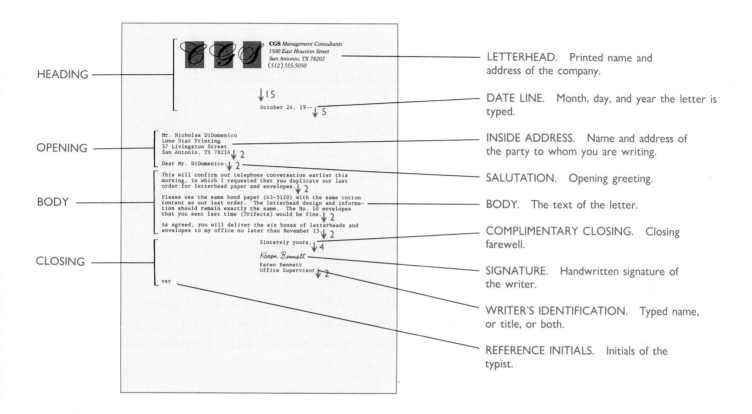

HEADING

LETTERHEAD. Printed name and address of the company.

DATE LINE. Month, day, and year the letter is typed.

OPENING

INSIDE ADDRESS. Name and address of the party to whom you are writing.

SALUTATION. Opening greeting.

BODY

BODY. The text of the letter.

COMPLIMENTARY CLOSING. Closing farewell.

CLOSING

SIGNATURE. Handwritten signature of the writer.

WRITER'S IDENTIFICATION. Typed name, or title, or both.

REFERENCE INITIALS. Initials of the typist.

26-G. FORMATTING A BUSINESS LETTER

Method 1: Using the Visual Guide. Detach Workguide page 37, the visual guide for letter placement. Read and follow the directions on the guide to correctly format business letters and to develop the judgment you need to estimate placement.

Method 2: Using a Placement Formula

1. For all letters use a 6-inch line (60 pica/70 elite). Set a tab stop at the center point.
2. Type the date on line 15 from the top of the paper, beginning at center.
3. Space down 5 lines, and type the inside address at the left margin on line 20.
4. Double-space before and after the salutation.

5. Single-space the body of the letter, but double-space between paragraphs.
6. Begin the complimentary closing at center, a double space below the body.
7. Begin the writer's identification at center, 4 lines below the complimentary closing.

Note: In order to make the letter appear centered on the page, you may adjust the number of blank lines—as few as 2 blank lines for a long letter to as many as 6 blank lines for a very short letter.

8. Type your initials at the left margin a double space below the last line of the writer's identification. Use lowercase letters without periods.

26-H. BUSINESS LETTERS

Complete Workguide pages 35–36 before typing the letters in this unit. Then, using the visual guide for letter placement on Workguide page 37 and the letterheads on Workguide pages 39 and 41, type the letters on the next page.

40-E. FORMATTING REVIEW

Before typing these jobs, review table typing (pages 69, 70, and 74), report typing (page 59), and letter typing (page 48) if necessary.

(page 59), and letter typing (page 48) if necessary.

TABLE 11
4-COLUMN TABLE

Spacing: single
Paper: plain, half sheet

QUARTERLY USED-CAR SALES				5
Lincoln Park Location				9
Type	July	August	September	14
Compact	43	34	50	16
Midsize	27	23	25	19
Luxury Sedan	17	21	14	22
Sports	9	7	16	24
Station Wagon	8	8	17	28

REPORT 10

Spacing: double
Paper: plain, full sheet

LINCOLN PARK SALES REPORT   5

Third Quarter, 19—   9

Sales at the Lincoln Park used-car lot for the third quarter of 19— were up 17.4 percent from the previous year. The total monthly auto sales were as follows: July, 104; August, 93; and September, 122. There appear to be two reasons for our success.   23 36 51 59

BUILDING AND LOT IMPROVEMENTS   65

After Saxton Auto Sales, Inc. purchased Lincoln Park in March, several landscaping and building renovation projects were implemented at our lot. The result has been an attractive location that promotes an atmosphere of quality and confidence.   80 93 108 114

INCREASE IN ADVERTISING   119

We think that the 43 percent increase in advertising expenditures since March has also paid dividends. This increase has been in the newspaper, radio, and television media.   132 146 153

We look forward to even better sales during the fourth quarter.   166

LETTER 13
MODIFIED-BLOCK STYLE

Paper: Workguide 65

When a letter has more than one enclosure, use the correct numeral and the word *Enclosures*. Example: *2 Enclosures*.

(Current date) / Mr. J. L. Payton, President / Saxton Auto Sales, Inc. / 3280 Ridge Street / Chicago Heights, IL 60411 / Dear Mr. Payton: 14 26

As members of the Saxton team, we at Lincoln Park are indeed proud to send you our sales report for the third quarter. The staff and I are pleased to be a part of your organization.   39 54 62

In addition to a copy of our sales report for the third quarter, a listing of sales by type of car for each of the months of July, August, and September is also enclosed.   77 92 96

Sincerely, / Tom J. Giesen / Sales Manager / *(Your initials)* / 2 Enclosures   105 106

Line: 6 inches (60 pica/70 elite)
Tab: center
Date: current
Paper: Workguide 39, 41

Leave I space between the state and the ZIP Code.

Standard punctuation: Colon after the salutation and comma after the complimentary closing.

LETTER 2
MODIFIED-BLOCK STYLE

Using the same date, body, and closing, retype Letter 1, addressing it to Mr. Charles LoPresti, Personnel Manager, Sunbelt Financial Services, 1335 Johnson Boulevard, Dallas, TX 75208.

CGS *Management Consultants*
1500 East Houston Street
San Antonio, TX 78202
(512) 555-5050

(Current Date)	4

Ms. Suzanne Dodds, President	10
Texas Business Forms, Inc.	15
15 South Walnut Street	19
Dallas, TX 75201	22

Dear Ms. Dodds:	25

Thank you for visiting our exhibit booth at the recent meeting   38
that was sponsored by the Texas Association for Training and   50
Development. We were extremely pleased with the number of   62
people who expressed an interest in our services.   72

We would like to invite you to a special session, designed to   84
provide more detailed information about our services, which we   97
are sponsoring for people from the Dallas area. The session   109
will be held on Tuesday, March 7, in Rayburn Hall of the   120
Dallas Convention Center. It will begin at 9 a.m.   130

If you would like to attend, please call my office for a   142
reservation. We would like you to be our guest at a luncheon   154
that will follow the morning session.   162

Sincerely yours,	165

Clifford G. Smiley	168
President	170

Type your own initials for the reference initials.

vsr	171

Business letter in modified-block style with (*a*) date and closing lines beginning at center, (*b*) all other lines beginning at left margin, and (*c*) single spacing.

TABLE, REPORT, AND LETTER REVIEW

Line: 60 spaces
Tab: 5, center
Spacing: single
Drills: 2 times
Workguide: 65
Format Guide: 29–30
Tape: 21A

Goals: To type 36 wam/3′/5e; to format a table, a report, and a letter.

40-A. WARMUP

S 1 He had a right to the profits from the two bushels of corn.
A 2 Fritz Krebs may join pushy crowds at quaint Texas villages.
N 3 She transferred from Flight 238 to Flight 749 at 10:56 p.m.

SKILLBUILDING

40-B. Take a 1-minute timing on the first paragraph to establish your base speed. Then take several 1-minute timings on the remaining paragraphs. As soon as you equal or exceed your base speed on one paragraph, advance to the next one.

40-B. SUSTAINED TYPING: SYMBOLS

4   It was quite normal that Patty was somewhat nervous as   12
5 she entered the college building. After four years of work   24
6 as a clerk, she was here to take the college entrance exam.   36

7   Just as you have likely done, Patty took her #2 pencil   12
8 and began to fill in the score sheet. A test administrator   24
9 (Mr. Gillam) had said that a grade of 75% would be passing.   36

10   Patty had come to Room #68 (a large lecture hall) from   12
11 the Ballou & Ingerham accounting firm. It's a "mighty long   24
12 hike," and almost 100% of the examinees were already there.   36

13   For a $25 fee, everyone in Room #68 (the <u>large</u> lecture   12
14 hall) answered the "carefully chosen" true-false questions.   24
15 About 40% had prepared by using Carr & Teugh's Study Guide.   36

| | | 2 | 3 | 4 | 5 | 6 | 7 | 8 | 9 | 10 | 11 | 12

40-C. DIAGNOSTIC TYPING: ALPHABET

Turn to the Diagnostic Typing: Alphabet routine at the back of the book. Take the Pretest, and record your performance on Workguide page 6. Then practice the drill lines for those reaches on which you made errors.

40-D. Spacing: double. Record your score.

40-D. SKILL MEASUREMENT: 3-MINUTE TIMED WRITING

16   Some of us can recall when a computer was a rare thing   12
17 in an office. Early models were huge and had quite limited   24
18 storage. It is hard to believe that things change so fast.   36
19   If we examine the uses of the early computers, we very   48
20 quickly realize that the processing of numbers was the only   60
21 activity. Use of computer jargon was in its early infancy.   72
22   The use of word processing is now one of the most com-   84
23 mon ways in which these giant tools are used. What a great   96
24 thing to have this pure magic at the tips of one's fingers.   108

| | | 2 | 3 | 4 | 5 | 6 | 7 | 8 | 9 | 10 | 11 | 12

Line: 60 spaces
Tab: 5
Spacing: single
Drills: 2 times
Workguide: 43–47
Format Guide: 15–18
Tape: 12B

LESSON
27

BUSINESS LETTERS

Goals: To improve speed and accuracy; to format business letters.

27-A. WARMUP

S 1 The eight men plan to go to the lake so that they can fish.
A 2 Because he was very lazy, Jack paid for six games and quit.
N 3 Order No. 3874 for $165.20 did not arrive until October 19.

SKILLBUILDING

PRETEST. Take a 1-minute timing; compute your speed and count errors.

27-B. PRETEST: CLOSE REACHES

4   We were hoping to agree on the need to check the value   12
5 of our assets. No one should be opposed to finding answers   24
6 that would give us our worth. Old records and ledgers will   36
7 be sorted, and we will unite in our effort to get the data.   48
   | | | 2 | 3 | 4 | 5 | 6 | 7 | 8 | 9 | 10 | 11 | 12

PRACTICE.
   Speed Emphasis: If you made 2 or fewer errors on the Pretest, type each line twice.
   Accuracy Emphasis: If you made 3 or more errors, type each group of lines (as though it were a paragraph) twice.

27-C. PRACTICE: ADJACENT KEYS

8 as ashes cases class asset astute passes chased creases ask
9 op optic ropes grope snoop oppose copied proper trooper top
10 we weave tweed towed weigh wealth twenty fewest answers wet
11 rt worth alert party smart artist sorted charts turtles art

27-D. PRACTICE: CONSECUTIVE FINGERS

12 sw sweet swarm swing swift switch answer swampy swims swirl
13 un undue bunch stung begun united punish outrun untie funny
14 gr grand agree angry grade growth egress hungry group graph
15 ol older solid tools spool volume evolve uphold olive scold

POSTTEST. Repeat the Pretest and compare performance.
27-F. The opening lines of a letter require the quick operation of the return key. Type these six opening lines 3 times as quickly as possible.

27-E. POSTTEST: CLOSE REACHES

27-F. PRODUCTION PRACTICE: LETTER PARTS

(Current Date) ↓5

Ms. Naomi Rodriquez
Rex Travel Agency
18 South Liberty Place
Ogden, UT 84401 ↓2

Dear Ms. Rodriquez:

27-G. BUSINESS LETTERS

Use the visual guide for letter placement on Workguide page 37 and the letterheads on Workguide pages 43–47 to type Letters 3–5 on page 51. Use a 6-inch line (60 pica/70 elite spaces) and the modified-block style illustrated on page 49.

TABLE 8
4-COLUMN TABLE

Spacing: single
Paper: plain, half sheet

TRI-CITIES BUSINESS SCHOOL   5

Home Backgrounds of Students, October 19--   14

Location	Men	Women	Total	
Farm	86	104	190	20
Small Town	83	59	142	24
Small City	175	166	341	27
Medium-Size City	384	372	756	32
Large City	92	134	226	36

Location — Men — Women — Total   18

TABLE 9
3-COLUMN TABLE

Spacing: double
Paper: plain, full sheet

AVERAGE GRAIN YIELDS   4

Chippewa County, 19—   8

Crop	Bushels Per Acre	Compared With Last Year	
Barley	55.0	106.8%	20
Corn	84.6	103.3%	23
Oats	71.9	98.6%	25
Soybeans	42.7	92.2%	29
Wheat	45.3	107.6%	32

Compared With   11
Last Year   17

TABLE 10
4-COLUMN TABLE

Spacing: double
Paper: plain, full sheet

Center and single-space each line of a two-line title. If possible, the first line should be longer than the second.

WORK STATUS OF STUDENTS AT   5
APEX BUSINESS SCHOOL   9

Enrollment and Work Status	1987	1988	1989	
Full-time student/no job	16%	12%	14%	23
Full-time student/part-time job	41%	46%	47%	31
Full-time student/full-time job	3%	4%	3%	39
Part-time student/no job	7%	4%	5%	45
Part-time student/part-time job	14%	16%	13%	53
Part-time student/full-time job	19%	18%	18%	61

Enrollment and Work Status   17

TITLES IN BUSINESS CORRESPONDENCE

Courtesy titles always precede an individual's name in the inside address of a letter; for example, *Mr., Mrs., Ms.,* or *Dr.* In the closing lines, however, a courtesy title does not precede a man's name; a woman may include a courtesy title in either her handwritten name or her typed name.

A job title may be typed on the same line as the person's name, on a line by itself, or on the same line as the company name, depending on which arrangement gives the best visual balance.

```
INSIDE ADDRESS:                CLOSING LINES:

                               Sincerely yours,
Mr. Joel Chiang, President     (Ms.) Pilar Figueroa
Fairweather Travel, Inc.
                               Pilar Figueroa
Dr. Maryellen B. Gorman        Loan Officer
Resident Physician
Westfield Medical Center       Cordially yours,

                               Kathy Troy
Ms. Charlotte Townfield
Manager, Grove Finances        Miss Kathy Troy, Manager
                               Personnel Department
```

LETTER 3
MODIFIED-BLOCK STYLE

Line: 6 inches (60 pica/70 elite)
Tab: center
Date: line 15
Paper: Workguide 43

(Current Date) / Mr. Raymond Bentley / Personnel Director / Adam — 12
Metal Products / P.O. Box 408 / Stillwater, OK 74074 / Dear Mr. Bentley: — 25

Thank you for responding to our advertisement regarding the special — 39
seminars we sponsor for supervisory and middle management personnel. — 52

We are in a position to provide a series of classes and/or seminars for — 67
the supervisors at your plant, or if you prefer, we can invite you to enroll — 82
selected supervisors at workshops that will be held in your area for — 96
individuals from various firms. — 102

I will call you next week to set up an appointment so that I can explain — 117
our programs and answer any questions you may have. — 127

Sincerely yours, / Clifford G. Smiley / President / *(Your Initials)* — 136

LETTER 4
MODIFIED-BLOCK STYLE

Paper: Workguide 45

(Current Date) / Ms. Dorothy Garcia, Manager / Kearfott Defense Sys- — 13
tems / 1130 Lee Highway / San Angelo, TX 76903 / Dear Ms. Garcia: — 25

Thank you for your complimentary letter concerning the seminars we — 38
sponsored for your supervisors last week. — 46

I plan to share your letter with our instructor, Mr. Edward Min. I know — 61
he will be delighted with the rating he received and with the comments — 75
that were included by some of the participants. — 85

I think that your suggestion for a follow-up seminar with Mr. Min is an — 99
excellent idea. I will call you early next month to discuss possible dates. — 114

Yours truly, / (Ms.) Luanne A. Chekarsky / Training Director / *(Your — 126
Initials)*

LETTER 5
MODIFIED-BLOCK STYLE

Paper: Workguide 47

(Current Date) / Mr. Charles McGinnis, President / Schiffenhaus, Inc. / — 14
61A Binghamton Place / Roswell, NM 88201 / Dear Mr. McGinnis: — 25

Use the same body and closing lines as in Letter 3. — 136

Line: 60 spaces
Tab: 5
Spacing: single
Drills: 2 times
Workguide: 64
Format Guide: 27–29
Tape: 20A

LESSON
39

TABLES WITH LONG CENTERED COLUMN HEADINGS

Goals: To improve speed and accuracy; to improve proofreading skills; to format long centered column headings.

39-A. WARMUP

S 1 Dick said that the next sign might be the one for the show.
A 2 Big Chuck Jarvey quoted amounts for extra prizes last week.
N 3 My balcony seats are those numbered 10, 29, 38, 47, and 56.

SKILLBUILDING

39-B. Type the paragraph and correct the errors.

39-B. PRODUCTION PRACTICE: PROOFREADING

4 All members of hte Toledoe Data Prosessors Association will
5 be asked ot vote next weak. Desisions will be made about a
6 merjer with the Toledoe PC Club. Speakers will present the
7 arguments for bot sides ofthe issue befor the members vote.

39-C. PROGRESSIVE PRACTICE: NUMBERS

Turn to the Progressive Practice: Numbers routine at the back of the book. Take several 30-second timings, starting at the point where you left off the last time. Record your progress on Workguide page 6.

39-D. FORMATTING TABLES WITH LONG CENTERED COLUMN HEADINGS

The table below illustrates three types of centered headings: short, long, and two-line.

LAKEVIEW MANOR APARTMENTS ↓ 2		
January 1, 19--, Rate Schedule ↓ 3		
Type of Unit	Number of Units	Monthly Rental Cost per Unit
Three bedrooms, three baths	24	$1,240.50
Two bedrooms, two baths	12	960.00
Two bedrooms, one bath	36	787.50
One bedroom, one bath	24	595.50
Studio, one bath	24	390.00

Short Centered Column Headings. The first one—the short centered column heading—is centered above the column as described in Lesson 38 on page 74 ($27 - 12 = 15$ and $15 \div 2 = 7\frac{1}{2}$; indent 7 spaces).

Long Centered Column Headings. The second column heading is longer than any of the column entries and is, therefore, part of the key line. To determine the horizontal placement of the column:

1. Subtract the number of spaces in the longest item in the column from the number of spaces in the column heading.
2. Divide the answer by 2 (drop any fraction), and indent the column that number of spaces. In the illustration, $15 - 2 = 13$ and $13 \div 2 = 6\frac{1}{2}$. Indent the column 6 spaces.

Two-Line Column Headings. The third column heading is so long that it requires two lines. Both lines are underscored, and the second one aligns horizontally with the other column headings. The shorter line is centered under the longer one ($19 - 8 = 11$ and $11 \div 2 = 5\frac{1}{2}$). Indent the second line of the heading 5 spaces.

Before typing Tables 8–10, complete Workguide page 64.

Line: 60 spaces
Tab: 5
Spacing: single
Drills: 2 times
Workguide: 49–51
Format Guide: 17–18
Tape: 12B

LESSON 28

BUSINESS LETTERS

Goals: To type 31 wam/3'/5e; to format business letters.

28-A. WARMUP

S 1 They may wish to help me fight the problem to the very end.
A 2 David quickly put the frozen jars away in small gray boxes.
N 3 Al's sales for the last month went from $35,786 to $41,290.

SKILLBUILDING

28-B. PROGRESSIVE PRACTICE: ALPHABET

Turn to the Progressive Practice: Alphabet routine at the back of the book. Take several 30-second timings, starting at the point where you left off the last time. Record your progress on Workguide page 5.

28-C. Take two 1-minute timings. The last two digits of each number provide a cumulative word count to help you determine your wam speed.

28-C. NUMBER TYPING

4 3801 4702 1803 9304 6305 8006 2807 3308 5909 6110 9011 1212
5 4813 1914 7915 5316 8117 2418 7619 3720 9421 5922 7023 2324
6 8825 4126 6827 3128 9629 7530 5831 2632 1733 8834 6235 4036
7 2737 8538 5539 1140 3941 4642 9943 6744 7345 8146 3947 5248

28-D. Type lines 8–11 twice each. Then take two 1-minute timings on lines 12–15.

28-D. SYMBOL TYPING

8 sws sw2s s2s s@s s2s@s s2@s frf fr4f f4f f$f f4f$f f4$f $44
9 lol lo9l 19l 1(1 19l(1 19(1 ded de3d d3d d#d d3d#d d3#d #33
10 ju7 ju7j j7j j&j j7j&j j7&j frf fr5f f5f f%f f5f%f f5%f 55%
11 ;p; ;p0; ;0; ;); ;0;); ;0); kik ki8k k8k k*k k8k*k k8*k ***
12 Invoice #3212 to Klekburg & Baines requested the following:
13 (1) 9 disks @ $2.60 each, (2) 7 tapes @ $2 each, (3) 8 pens
14 @ $1.10 each, and 18 records @ $6 each. The total for this
15 bill is $154.20, with a 7% sales tax adding another $10.79.

28-E. Spacing: double. Record your score.

28-E. SKILL MEASUREMENT: 3-MINUTE TIMED WRITING

16   Have you ever heard it said that attitude can help you   12
17 achieve a higher altitude than your aptitude? Just think a   24
18 minute about what this is implying.   31
19   It is still essential that you acquire many skills and   43
20 that you learn all the important concepts and principles of   55
21 the career that you might pursue.   62
22   Keep in mind, though, that experts say that it is your   74
23 attitude that helps you get to the top. How do you size up   86
24 when one evaluates your attitude?   93

| 1 | 2 | 3 | 4 | 5 | 6 | 7 | 8 | 9 | 10 | 11 | 12 |

38-E. FORMATTING TABLES WITH SHORT CENTERED COLUMN HEADINGS

Tables with short centered column headings are formatted almost like those with blocked column headings, as described on page 71: (1) Select the key line. (2) Backspace-center to set the left margin. (3) Space across to set the column tabs.

To compute the number of spaces that each column heading should be indented from the start of its column:

1. Subtract the number of spaces in the column heading from the number of spaces in the longest item of the column.
2. Divide the answer by 2 (drop any fraction), and indent the column heading that number of spaces.

The computations shown here are for the two column headings illustrated at the right:

Column 1: 18 − 4 = 14; 14 ÷ 2 = 7; indent the heading 7 spaces.

Column 2: 12 − 5 = 7; 7 ÷ 2 = 3½; indent the heading 3 spaces.

You may want to pencil in each indention reminder on the copy as shown so that you will not forget to indent.

```
        COMPANY PRESIDENTS
                          ↓3

  7⌋Name              3⌋Years
                          ↓2
  John A. Price          1946-1953
  William P. Hocking     1954-1968
  Roberto S. Ojeda       1969-1984
  Carol E. Herndon       1985-Present
```

Short centered column headings are capitalized, underscored, preceded by 2 blank lines, and followed by 1 blank line.

TABLE 6
3-COLUMN TABLE WITH
SHORT COLUMN HEADINGS

Spacing: double
Paper: plain, half sheet

The $ sign is not repeated in a column of figures.

WP Most word processing software has a decimal tab feature that aligns the decimal points in a column of figures.

TOP UNITED WAY CONTRIBUTORS			5
Department	Leader	Amount	10
Purchasing	Kellee A. Dillon	$3,073.00	17
Operations and Maintenance	Gregory J. Hulbert	2,979.25	27
Research and Development	Mary L. Nardi	2,482.50	36
Shipping	Robert C. Higgins	2,146.00	43
Accounting	John P. Touchinski	1,850.60	50
Publications	Clarence L. Roth	1,752.60	57
Sales	Paulette L. Skehen	1,467.00	63

TABLE 7
3-COLUMN TABLE WITH
SHORT COLUMN HEADINGS

Spacing: double
Paper: plain, half sheet

WP Some word processors have a column-layout feature that automatically aligns column headings with the column entries.

ASHTON PUBLISHING			3
Print Titles for December 19—			9
Title	Author	Editor	13
Emerging Mutual Funds	Bernadette M. Chow	Maria A. Sartorelli	24
The Glitter of Gold	Lester A. Frazier	Paul J. Spalding	35
Guide to Buying Stocks	Alfred E. Hughes	Joan G. Valentine	46
A Model Portfolio	Kimberly Ferns Ewing	Pablo J. Menendez	57
Selecting a Home Mortgage	Mike D. Reynolds	Sharon B. Dohrman	68
Starting Your Own Business	Elise M. Harrington	Philip L. Knox	80

LETTER 6
MODIFIED-BLOCK STYLE

Paper: Workguide 49

28-F. BUSINESS LETTERS

Use the date April 15 to type this letter from Luanne A. Chekarsky / Training Director. Send the letter to Ms. Charlotte Luna / Personnel Manager / Wilmont Financial Securities / 1575 Longhorn Boulevard / Corpus Christi, TX 78402 / (Supply a salutation and closing lines.)

In reviewing my records, I note that we submitted	10
a proposal to you on March 15 to conduct two seminars	21
for your administrative support personnel during the	31
week of June 24.	35
If you are still interested in having these workshops,	46
please let me know within the next two weeks so	55
that I can schedule the speaker and prepare the	65
necessary materials.	69
If I do not hear from you by May 1, I will	77
assume that you no longer wish to sponsor the	87
seminar at this time. If you have any questions or	97
need further information, please don't hesitate to call me.	109

LETTER 7
MODIFIED-BLOCK STYLE

Paper: Workguide 51

Use the date April 15 to type this letter from Clifford G. Smiley / President. Send the letter to Mr. Wayne Johnson / Johnson Travel Agency / 1107 Cedarcrest Avenue / San Antonio, TX 78204 / Dear Wayne: / (Supply an appropriate closing.)

I am delighted that you will be able to make	9
arrangements for our company-sponsored trip to Hawaii	20
during the second week of July. As I indicated to	30
you on the phone, this trip is an incentive bonus for	41
employees who demonstrated consistently superior performance	53
during the last 12 months.	58
Enclosed are the names and addresses of the individuals	69
who have won this recognition. The group will leave together	82
from the local airport. I understand that there will be	93
one stop in Los Angeles on the way to Honolulu. Is that	105
correct?	106
When you have all the information regarding time of	117
departure and hotel reservations, please call me so that	128
I can stop by to discuss the arrangements with you.	138

Note: To indicate that an item is enclosed with a letter, type the word *Enclosure* a single space below the reference initials of a business letter. Example:
urs
Enclosure

Insert an enclosure notation in the closing lines.

TABLES WITH SHORT CENTERED COLUMN HEADINGS

Line: 60 spaces
Tab: 5
Spacing: single
Drills: 2 times
Format Guide: 27
Tape: 19A

Goals: To type 35 wam/3'/5e; to format tables with short centered column headings.

38-A. WARMUP

S 1 They will take their rowboat when they go back to the lake.
A 2 Mac Wiker did prize the five or six big quarterly journals.
N 3 Nina said that 27 of the 30 clients had read pages 491-568.

SKILLBUILDING

38-B. SUSTAINED TYPING: NUMBERS

38-B. Take a 1-minute timing on the first paragraph to establish your base speed. Then take several 1-minute timings on the remaining paragraphs. As soon as you equal or exceed your base speed on one paragraph, advance to the next one.

4   Michael learned through firsthand experience last week 12
5 that the cost of a week on the water can vary a great deal. 24
6 He says that a rowboat would be about right for his wallet. 36

7   His Uncle Bob told him that when he was his age he had 12
8 rented a small cabin for the huge sum of $105 for one week. 24
9 For $23 more, he rented a small boat and an outboard motor. 36

10   Then Uncle Bob went on to say that when he rented that 12
11 same cabin last year the cost had gone up to either $395 or 24
12 $410. The boat and motor rentals now cost from $62 to $87. 36

13   Aunt Kate said that she and her husband will be paying 12
14 either $1,946 or $2,073 for one week's sailing on a 53-foot 24
15 yacht. The boat has a 4-person crew and was built in 1982. 36

  | 1 | 2 | 3 | 4 | 5 | 6 | 7 | 8 | 9 | 10 | 11 | 12

38-C. PROGRESSIVE PRACTICE: ALPHABET

Turn to the Progressive Practice: Alphabet routine at the back of the book. Take several 30-second timings, starting at the point where you left off the last time. Record your progress on Workguide page 6.

38-D. SKILL MEASUREMENT: 3-MINUTE TIMED WRITING

38-D. Spacing: double. Record your score.

16   Each office has its own plan which is used for storing 12
17 and retrieving written information. This process is called 24
18 filing. All of us realize that things do differ because of 36
19 differences in offices, but the basic approach is the same. 48
20   A good filing system can help to make your office more 60
21 efficient. If you know where your documents are located, a 72
22 great deal of time can be saved. This time can be used for 84
23 the myriad of extra office jobs. Quick and easy access are 96
24 things to look for in a good records system. 105

  | 1 | 2 | 3 | 4 | 5 | 6 | 7 | 8 | 9 | 10 | 11 | 12

PERSONAL-BUSINESS LETTERS

Line: 60 spaces
Tab: 5
Spacing: single
Drills: 2 times
Format Guide: 17–20
Tape: 13B

Goals: To improve speed and accuracy; to format personal-business letters.

29-A. WARMUP

S 1 Go to the mall and see what might be the problem with Todd.
A 2 Two sax players in the jazz band gave a quick demo for Tom.
N 3 Seats 30, 31, 47, 48, 56, and 57 in Section 29 were unsold.

SKILLBUILDING

29-B. PROGRESSIVE PRACTICE: NUMBERS

Turn to the Progressive Practice: Numbers routine at the back of the book. Take several 30-second timings, starting at the point where you left off the last time. Record your progress on Workguide page 5.

29-C. Take a 1-minute timing on the first paragraph to establish your base speed. Then take successive 1-minute timings on the other paragraphs. As soon as you equal or exceed your base speed on one paragraph, advance to the next one.

29-C. SUSTAINED TYPING: SYLLABIC INTENSITY

4　　There are many types of buyers to be found in society.　12
5　One common type is known as the bargain hound. This person　24
6　goes all out to find items marked below the sticker prices.　36

7　　Another type of consumer is called an emotional buyer.　12
8　Buying decisions are made with the heart, not the head. It　24
9　seems this buyer is trying to buy a feeling, not an object.　36

10　　A third type of consumer that can be identified is the　12
11　compulsive shopper. This buyer doesn't really need what is　24
12　purchased but continually desires to go on shopping binges.　36

13　　The sensible shopper has the advantage over the others　12
14　described. This shopper establishes a dollar limit for the　24
15　needed purchases and then compares store prices for values.　36

　| 1 | 2 | 3 | 4 | 5 | 6 | 7 | 8 | 9 | 10 | 11 | 12

29-D. The closing lines of a letter require the quick operation of the return and tab keys. Type these closing lines 3 times as quickly as possible.

Tab: center

29-D. PRODUCTION PRACTICE: LETTER PARTS

TAB → 　Sincerely yours,
　　　　　　　　　　↓4

TAB → 　Thomas C. Butler
TAB → 　Personnel Manager
　　　　　　　　　　↓2

urs
Enclosure

TABLE 3
3-COLUMN TABLE

Spacing: double
Paper: plain, full sheet

STOCK MARKET GROUPS WITH LARGEST GAINS ↓2   8

For Quarter Ending March 31, 19-- ↓3   14

No.	Leading Industries	Leading Company ↓2	
			21
1	Retail–Discount	Marco, Inc.	27
2	Retail–Clothing	Fairview Stores	33
3	Personal Services	Liv-Rite Dynamics	40
4	Drug Manufacturers	Cleveland International	48
5	Shoe Manufacturers	Kise Leather Company	56
6	Retail–Gift Specialty	Dahlstrom Brothers	64

TABLE 4
3-COLUMN TABLE

Spacing: double
Paper: plain, full sheet

SUPERIOR INVESTMENTS ↓2   4

Five-Year Share Price Comparisons ↓3   11

Mutual Fund	1984	1989 ↓2	
			14
Superior Growth	11.08	32.84	19
Superior High Yield	23.87	42.38	25
Superior Income	53.61	96.35	30
Superior International	48.32	54.72	37
Superior Tax-Free Bond	35.78	69.06	43
Superior Technology	13.81	18.56	49
Superior Utilities	49.02	55.79	54

TABLE 5
3-COLUMN TABLE

Spacing: double
Paper: plain, full sheet

SUGGESTED READING LIST   4

Title	Author	Publisher	
			8
The Great Depression	Willard P. McCarty	Econ Press	18
The Postwar Boom	Bonnie F. Meinert	Ashton Publishing	28
War and the Economy	Wanda M. Dellies	Dobsons, Inc.	38
The Mid-80s Bear	Laura L. Ohman	Cierra Books	46
Recession in the 1970s	Robert J. Sachs	Scanlon Publishers	57
Inflation Theories	James D. Wilson Jr.	Cordero & Sons	67
The New Economists	K. V. Fung	Collegiate Books	76

29-E. FORMATTING PERSONAL-BUSINESS LETTERS

Personal-business letters are written to conduct one's own personal-business affairs. Since they are typed on plain paper, the writer's return address must be included as part of the letter. In the illustration below, the return address is typed below the name in the closing lines. This style, although not the traditional one, is becoming increasingly popular. In the more conventional style, the writer's address is typed above the date on lines 13 and 14. Reference initials are not used with either format.

LETTER 8
PERSONAL-BUSINESS LETTER IN
MODIFIED-BLOCK STYLE

Line: 6 inches (60 pica/70 elite)
Tab: center
Date: line 15
Paper: plain

If a letter is addressed to a company rather than to an individual, the appropriate salutation is *Ladies and Gentlemen* or *Gentlemen.*

Reference initials are not needed in letters you type for yourself.

|15

(Current Date)   4
|5

Gonzales Investment Services   10
15 Plainfield Avenue   14
Ft. Lauderdale, FL 33302   18

Ladies and Gentlemen: 23

Your advertisement in today's newspaper is of great interest   35
to me. I have a certificate of deposit that will be maturing   47
in another six weeks, and I am considering the various   58
investment options that are open to me.   66

The ad states that you have a service available whereby a   78
representative from your firm will do a complete financial   89
analysis free of charge. I am interested in having such an   101
analysis done. Since I have a full-time job, it would be   113
necessary to have an evening appointment.   121

Please have someone call me at 555-8407 to arrange a time that 134
would be convenient. I am usually home from work by 6 p.m.   146
every day. ↓2   148

                          Sincerely yours, |4   151

                          (Miss) Karen S. Rinaldi   156
                          156 Pleasantview Drive   160
                          Dania, FL 33004   163

LETTER 9
PERSONAL-BUSINESS LETTER IN
MODIFIED-BLOCK STYLE

Paper: plain

Using the same return address, date, body, and closing lines, retype Letter 8, addressing it to Mr. Roger Allgor / Empire Financial Services / 75 Canfield Avenue / Hollywood, FL 33003 / Dear Mr. Allgor:

Line: 60 spaces
Tab: 5
Spacing: single
Drills: 2 times
Format Guide: 25–27
Tape: 18A

LESSON 37

TABLES WITH BLOCKED COLUMN HEADINGS

Goals: To improve speed and accuracy; to format tables with blocked column headings.

37-A. WARMUP

S 1 They caught the last boat back to the mainland at the dock.
A 2 Fay's wipers quit just when Marv locked the zoo's gate box.
N 3 The left-hand keys are 12345, and the right ones are 67890.

SKILLBUILDING

PRETEST. Take a 1-minute timing; compute your speed and count errors.

37-B. PRETEST: VERTICAL REACHES

4   Some lawmakers in Washington attribute our basic bank-   12
5 ing success to judicious or scientific cash reserve manage-   24
6 ment. A bank just cannot be drawn into dropping its guard.   36

  | | | 2 | 3 | 4 | 5 | 6 | 7 | 8 | 9 | 10 | 11 | 12

PRACTICE.
   Speed Emphasis: If you made 2 or fewer errors on the Pretest, type each line twice.
   Accuracy Emphasis: If you made 3 or more errors on the Pretest, type lines 7–14 once; then repeat.

37-C. PRACTICE: UP REACHES

7 at atlas plate water later batch fatal match late gate atom
8 dr draft drift drums drawn drain drama dress drab drag drop
9 ju jumpy juror junky jumbo juice julep judge just judo jump
10 es essay press bless crest quest fresh rises less best pest

37-D. PRACTICE: DOWN REACHES

11 ca cable cabin cadet camel cameo candy carve cash case cane
12 nk trunk drink rinks prank brink drank crank sink monk bank
13 ba batch badge bagel baked banjo barge basis bank back bass
14 sc scale scald scrub scalp scare scout scarf scan scar scat

POSTTEST. Repeat the Pretest and compare performance.

37-E. POSTTEST: VERTICAL REACHES

37-F. FORMATTING TABLES WITH BLOCKED COLUMN HEADINGS

Underscored column headings are used to identify the information in the columns. Blocked headings (as shown at the right) are becoming increasingly popular because they are quick and easy to format. The first column heading begins at the left margin. The second column heading begins at the tab setting for the second column, and so on.

When items are selected for the key line, the column heading is considered as one of the column entries; that is, it is selected for the key line if it is the longest entry in the column.

Follow the steps for formatting a table outlined on page 70.

SILICON VALLEY LODGING, INC.

November 1, 19--
↓3

Name of Motel	City	Rooms
Rainbow Motel	Cupertino	114
Red Horse Ranch	Los Gatos	53
Airport Motel	San Jose	78
Friendship Inn	Santa Clara	96
Kamdahl's Motel	Sunnyvale	102

↓2

Key Line: Red Horse Ranch₁₂₃₄₅₆Santa Clara₁₂₃₄₅₆Rooms

Line: 60 spaces
Tab: 5, center
Spacing: single
Drills: 2 times
Workguide: 53–55
Format Guide: 19–20
Tape: 13B

LESSON
30

LETTER REVIEW

Goals: To type 32 wam/3'/5e; to format personal-business and business letters.

30-A. WARMUP

S 1 The bills from last week came in the mail at the same time.
A 2 Zeb gave Holly six dozen pears to make two quarts of juice.
N 3 Our sales for May increased $13,470, to a total of $98,652.

SKILLBUILDING

30-B. Take three 12-second timings on each line. The scale gives your wam speed for each 12-second timing.

30-B. 12-SECOND SPRINTS

J 4 John just enjoyed a jitney ride with Jerry, Joan, and Jeff.
Q 5 Quincy was not quite equal to quoting the quip from Quebec.
Z 6 Zeblin was dazzled by the size of the prize for the puzzle.

　　　5　　10　　15　　20　　25　　30　　35　　40　　45　　50　　55　　60

30-C. Use the shift lock when a word or series of words is typed in all caps.

30-C. TECHNIQUE TYPING: SHIFT/CAPS LOCK

7   Send the package to CRANE TRAVEL AGENCY in SPRINGFIELD, IL.
8   The SAILING CARRIER leaves MIAMI every Saturday in OCTOBER.
9   They REQUEST that the DEBIT MEMO be sent by MARCH 15, 1992.
10 ANN PAIGE got the leading part of ISABELLE in MY HOME TOWN.

30-D. PRODUCTION PRACTICE: LINE-ENDING DECISIONS

The skill measurement timed writing in 28-E on page 52 is shown on a 60-space line. Set your margins for a 40-space line, and type the three paragraphs, deciding for yourself where to end each line. Listen for the bell; *do not look up.* After typing the paragraphs on a 40-space line, change your margins for a 50-space line and repeat the exercise.

30-E. Spacing: double. Record your score.

30-E.   SKILL MEASUREMENT: 3-MINUTE TIMED WRITING

　　　　　　　1　　　　　　2　　　　　　3　　　　　　4
11　　　When you start a new office job, strive to learn about   12
　　　　5　　　　　　　6　　　　　　7　　　　　　8
12　the flow of work as quickly as possible. Explore how forms   24
　　　　　　9　　　　　　10
13　and letters are processed and handled.   32
　　　11　　　　　　12　　　　　　13　　　　　　14
14　　　One way to learn about the flow of work is to consider   44
　　　15　　　　　　16　　　　　　17　　　　　　18
15　the roles that are played by each office worker. Strive to   56
　　　19　　　　　　20　　　　　　21
16　learn about the work done by each one.   64
　　　　　22　　　　　　23　　　　　　24　　　　　　25
17　　　Think through how work is done in your office. If you   76
　　　26　　　　　　27　　　　　　28　　　　　　29
18　take time to analyze who does what and in what order, it is   88
　　　30　　　　　　31　　　　　　32
19　likely that you will be a good worker.   96

　| | | 2 | 3 | 4 | 5 | 6 | 7 | 8 | 9 | 10 | 11 | 12

36-E. FORMATTING A TABLE

Before you begin, clear all tabs and move the margins to the extreme left and right.

1. Select the Key Line. The key line consists of the longest item in each column, plus 6 blank spaces for each open area between columns.

2. Set the Left Margin. From the center, backspace once for every 2 characters or spaces in the key line, and set the left margin at the point to which you have backspaced.

Example: se/nt/en/ce/12/34/56/th/ou/gh/12/34/56/ta/bl/es

Note: Do not backspace for an extra stroke at the end of the line.

3. Set Tabs. Space across the paper once for *each* letter and *each* space in the longest entry of the first column plus the 6 blank spaces, and set a tab for the second column. Do the same for the longest entry in the second column plus the 6 blank spaces, and set a tab for the third column.

4. Compute the Top Margin. To center the table vertically, subtract the number of lines (including blank lines) in the table from either 66 (a full sheet of paper) or 33 (a half sheet) and divide by 2. If a fraction is left, drop it.

Example: 33 − 12 = 21; 21 ÷ 2 = 10½; begin typing on line 10.

5. Type the Table. Backspace-center the title in all-capital letters. Then leave 2 blank lines and type the body.

Note: Use the tab key to move across from column to column.

Practice. Center this double-spaced table on a half sheet.

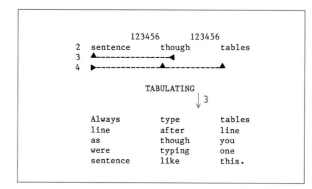

Before typing Tables 1 and 2, complete Workguide page 63.

36-F. TABLES

Type Tables 1 and 2 on half sheets of paper, double-spacing the body of each table. Leave the machine on single spacing until you are ready to begin typing the column entries.

Remember to clear all tab stops and to move the margins to the extreme left and right before formatting each table.

TABLE 1
3-COLUMN TABLE

Spacing: double
Paper: plain, half sheet

Number columns with decimals align on the decimal point.

	FIRST-QUARTER SALES ↓2 As a Percentage of Target Goal ↓3		
			4
			10
Connecticut	Malcolm W. Tarsun	106.5	16
New Jersey	Ingrid S. Torgeson	112.2	23
New York	Elise R. Estivant	98.3	29
Pennsylvania	J. D. Greenberg	104.7	35

Key Line: Pennsylvania₁₂₃₄₅₆Ingrid S. Torgeson₁₂₃₄₅₆106.5

TABLE 2
2-COLUMN TABLE

Spacing: double
Paper: plain, half sheet

	ANNIVERSARY PLANNING COMMITTEE	
		6
M. Choy	Human Resources	10
J. Ortega	Quality Control	15
D. Pierce	Mail Services	20
J. West	Accounts Receivable	25

30-F. LETTER REVIEW

Assignment	Style	Special Instructions	Words
Letter 10 Plain Paper	Personal-Business	Arrange as shown below, with return address after the writer's identification.	184
Letter 11 Workguide: 53	Modified-Block	Omit return address; add your reference initials.	174
Letter 12 Workguide: 55	Modified-Block	Same as Letter 11, except add this final sentence to paragraph 3: "As a token of my appreciation for the work already done, please accept the enclosed centennial certificate." Add your reference initials and an enclosure notation.	197

LETTER 10
PERSONAL-BUSINESS LETTER IN
MODIFIED-BLOCK STYLE

WP

If you had typed Letter 10 on a word processor, the only part that you would have to type for Letter 11 would be the reference initials (you would also need to delete the return address). The body and closing lines would not need to be retyped.

(Current Date)   4

Ms. ~~Judith~~ *Jolene* Durish, President   10
Flair Entertainment Company   15
15 South Montrose ~~Street~~   20
Pasadena, CA 91103   23

Dear Ms. Durish: 27

The information you ~~provided~~ *forwarded to* me concerning the possibility of   40
providing "The Leading Edge" for a concert at our upcoming   52
celebration is *very* much appreciated.   59

After consulting with members of ~~the~~ *our* planning committee and   71
checking our financial status for this event, we have decided   83
that we would like to explore this with you further. Could   95
you ~~arrange~~ *plan* to meet with a group of our committee members? We   107
meet every Thursday evening from 7 to 10 p.m. Please let me   119
know what would be convenient ~~Friday~~ *Thursday* night for you.   130

We ~~will~~ look forward to meeting with you and to possibly   140
making final arrangements for booking "The Leading Edge" as   152
the main attraction at the celebration of our town's   163
centennial.   165

                          Sincerely yours,   168

                          Peter Lazzaro, Chairperson   173
                          Pomona Centennial
                          15 Greenmont Terrace   182
                          Pomona, CA 91702   185

LESSON
36

TABLES

Line: 60 spaces
Tab: 5
Spacing: single
Drills: 2 times
Workguide: 63
Format Guide: 25
Tape: 17A

Goals: To type 35 wam/3'/5e; to format 2- and 3-column tables.

36-A. WARMUP

S 1 Fritz saw many old jets at the air show held in the spring.
A 2 Jim kept Gil away because four dozen taxi drivers had quit.
N 3 Tickets were incorrectly numbered from 49801 through 53762.

SKILLBUILDING

36-B. PACED PRACTICE

Turn to the Paced Practice routine at the back of the book. Take several 2-minute timings, starting at the point where you left off the last time. Record your progress on Workguide page 6.

36-C. Spacing: double. Record your score.

36-C. SKILL MEASUREMENT: 3-MINUTE TIMED WRITING

```
                 1                2              3            4
4        You have to realize that your phone work can be a real    12
              5              6            7            8
5    plus for your firm's image.  Don't jabber like some do when   24
           9            10          11
6    on the phone, as some customer might react negatively.        35
         12          13          14          15
7        It is important to answer the telephone graciously, as    47
       16          17          18        19
8    this conveys a positive image for your company.  The caller   59
       20          21          22          23
9    must be aware that the correct party has been reached.        70
           24          25          26          27
10       A friendly greeting will help to put a caller at ease.    82
       28          29          30          31
11   Next, you should state the name of the company and your own   94
           32          33          34          35
12   name.  Have references handy for those hard questions.       105

     |  |  2  |  3  |  4  |  5  |  6  |  7  |  8  |  9  | 10  | 11  | 12
```

36-D. BASIC PARTS OF A TABLE

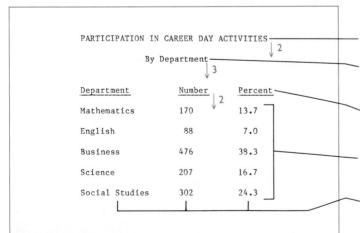

TITLE. Identifies contents of table. Center and type in all-capital letters.

SUBTITLE. Sometimes used to give more information about the table. Center a double space below the title, with the first and all principal words capitalized.

COLUMN HEADINGS. Tell what is in each column. Either begin at left of column or center over the column. Underscore, and leave 2 blank lines before and 1 blank line after.

BODY. Consists of the columns in the table. Center horizontally, usually with 6 spaces between columns; may be either single-spaced or double-spaced.

COLUMN. Is a listing of information. Word columns align at the left. Columns of whole numbers align at the right; columns of decimal amounts align on the decimal point.

LESSON
31
ONE-PAGE REPORTS

Line: 60 spaces
Tab: 5
Spacing: single
Drills: 2 times
Workguide: 57–60
Format Guide: 21–22
Tape: 14B

Goals: To improve speed and accuracy; to use proofreaders' marks; to format a one-page report.

31-A. WARMUP

S 1 Jaime said that the rich man may fix the pens if they leak.
A 2 Godfrey monopolized conversations with six quite bad jokes.
N 3 Exactly 604 were bought and 523 sold at that store in 1987.

SKILLBUILDING

PRETEST. Take a 1-minute timing; compute your speed and count errors.

31-B. PRETEST: ALTERNATE- AND ONE-HAND WORDS

4   The chairman of the committee will handle the downtown   12
5 tax problem. If they reverse their earlier opinion, social   24
6 pressures might affect the way future problems are handled.   36
    | 1 | 2 | 3 | 4 | 5 | 6 | 7 | 8 | 9 | 10 | 11 | 12

PRACTICE.
   Speed Emphasis: If you made 2 or fewer errors on the Pretest, type each line twice.
   Accuracy Emphasis: If you made 3 or more errors, type each group of lines (as though it were a paragraph) 2 times.

31-C. PRACTICE: ALTERNATE HANDS

7 of the with girl right blame handle island antique chairman
8 is for wish town their panel formal social problem downtown
9 if sit work make tight amend profit eighty element neighbor
10 it pan busy they flair signs thrown theory signals problems

31-D. PRACTICE: ONE HAND

11 gas lip fact yolk taxes yummy affect poplin reverse pumpkin
12 far you cast kill draws jumpy grease uphill wagered opinion
13 tea pin cage lump beard hilly served limply bravest minimum
14 fat hip tree only great bully garage unhook reserve million

POSTTEST: Repeat the Pretest and compare performance.

31-E. POSTTEST: ALTERNATE- AND ONE-HAND WORDS

31-F. Set tabs every 12 spaces. Use the tab key to go from column to column. Type only once.

31-F. TECHNIQUE TYPING: TAB KEY

15 assets	awning	basket	blinds	boiler
16 breeze	bucket	canary	center	cinder
17 clocks	convoy	custom	debate	desert
18 detail	docket	effort	embryo	fiance
19 gopher	houses	icicle	jewels	knight
20 ladder	master	notion	optics	pantry
21 piracy	pencil	quarry	rating	riddle
22 saddle	senior	tennis	ticket	upward
23 violin	weaver	xylene	yeoman	zither

35-D. FORMATTING A REPORT WITH AN ENUMERATION AND A BIBLIOGRAPHY

Read Report 8 for the information it contains. Then carefully follow the instructions at the left, noting that the tab must be reset for the single-spaced numbered items.

REPORT 8
REPORT WITH ENUMERATION

Tab: 5, center
Spacing: double

The lines for each numbered item are single-spaced. However, double spacing is used between items.

Turnover lines are indented 4 spaces.

PREPARING A BIBLIOGRAPHY   5

By Heidi Keltjen   8

¶ A bibliography is *an alphabetic* listing of sources and is placed at the   22
end of the report, following these guide lines.   32

1. Use the *report* length line: 60 pica or 70 elite spaces.   44

2. Center the title in all-capital letters on line 13.   55
    Two ~~three~~ blank lines precede the body.   62

3. Arrange book information in ~~in~~ this order: *author,* title,   74
    publisher, place of publication, and date.   82

4. Arrange information for journals *articles* in this order: 94
    author, title of article (in quotation marks), title of   105
    journal (underscored), series number, volume number,   116
    issue number, date, and page number or numbers.   125

REPORT 9
BIBLIOGRAPHY

Tab: 5
Spacing: single

Organization as author

Book by one author

Article—no author

Book by two authors

Article by three or more authors
(*et al.* means "and others")

Article by one author

BIBLIOGRAPHY   2
↓3

Distributive Education Clubs of America, <u>Preparing for the</u>   14
    <u>Job Interview</u>, Educational Association Clearinghouse,   25
    San Francisco, 1981.   29

Faux, Marian, <u>The Executive Interview</u>, St. Martin's Press,   41
    New York, 1985.   44

"How They Sell to You Is How They'll Sell for You," <u>Sales &</u>   56
    <u>Marketing Management</u>, Vol. CXXXIII, No. 3, August 13,   67
    1984, pp. 77-78.   70

Meyer, Mary Coeli, and Inge M. Berchtold, <u>Getting the Job:</u>   82
    <u>How to Interview Successfully</u>, Petrocelli Books,   92
    Princeton, N.J., 1982.   96

Scott, Richard A., et al., "On-Campus Recruiting: The Stu-   108
    dents Speak Up," <u>Journal of Accountancy</u>, Vol. CLIX,   118
    No. 1, January 1985, pp. 60-62.   124

Solomon, Robert J., "Using the Interview in Small Business,"   136
    <u>Journal of Small Business Management</u>, Vol. XXII,   146
    No. 4, October 1984, pp. 17-23.   152

31-G. BASIC PARTS OF A REPORT

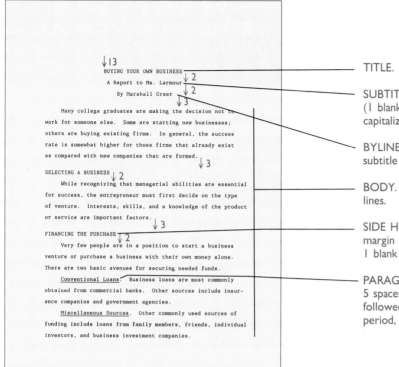

TITLE. Subject of the report; centered and typed in all-capital letters.

SUBTITLE. Secondary or explanatory title; centered a double space (1 blank line) below the title, with first and principal words capitalized.

BYLINE. Name of the writer; centered a double space below the subtitle or, if no subtitle is used, a double space below the title.

BODY. Text of the report; separated from the heading by 2 blank lines.

SIDE HEADING. Major subdivision of the report; typed at the left margin in all-capital letters; preceded by 2 blank lines and followed by 1 blank line.

PARAGRAPH HEADING. Minor subdivision of the report; indented 5 spaces, with first and principal words capitalized; underscored and followed by a period. (The spaces between the words, but not the period, are also underscored.)

31-H. FORMATTING A ONE-PAGE REPORT

Line Length. 6 inches (60 pica/70 elite).
Tab Stops. Always set two—one for indenting paragraphs and one for centering titles and subtitles.
Top Margin. 2 inches; center the title on line 13.
Spacing. Double-space the title block (title, subtitle, and byline) and the body of the report. Leave 2 blank lines (a triple space) between the title block and the body.
Bottom Reminder. Before inserting the paper, pencil in two very light lines (to be erased later): one line about an inch from the bottom to indicate where the last line of typing

should go, and a second line about an inch higher to serve as a warning.
Note: The easiest way to format a report is to use a *visual guide*—a sheet on which the margins are marked off in heavy lines. When this sheet is placed behind the paper on which you will type, the ruled lines show through to indicate the correct placement of margins and copy. Workguide pages 59 and 60 are visual guides for use in formatting reports.

Before typing Report 1, complete Workguide pages 57–58.

31-I. PROOFREADERS' MARKS

The proofreaders' marks shown below are used by writers and typists to indicate the changes to be made in typed copy when it is being revised for final typing. These marks are used in the report on the next page.

Proofreaders' Mark		Draft	Final Copy	Proofreaders' Mark		Draft	Final Copy
⌢	Omit space	blue bird	bluebird	∧	Insert word	she may ∧ go (*not*)	she may not go
∽	Transpose	which (will/you)	which you will	⧸	Delete	a rough draft	a draft
¶	Paragraph	¶ Most of the	Most of the	≡	Capitalize	Norwood street	Norwood Street

ENUMERATIONS AND BIBLIOGRAPHIES

Line: 60 spaces
Tab: 5, center
Spacing: single
Drills: 2 times
Format Guide: 23–26
Tape: 16A

Goals: To improve speed and accuracy; to improve word-division skills; to improve the skill of formatting from rough-draft copy; to format a report with an enumeration and a bibliography.

35-A. WARMUP

S 1 Pam lost an ax at the first lake when she went there today.
A 2 He picked two extra biology quizzes for Marv, Jan, and Hal.
N 3 The population of the city had grown by 237,645 since 1980.

SKILLBUILDING

35-B. Select the words that can be divided, and type them with a hyphen to show where the division should be (example: *fore-front*).

35-B. PRODUCTION PRACTICE: WORD DIVISION

4	brought	account	business
5	divide	haven't	borderline
6	weekly	USMC	thrilled
7	isn't	knowledge	TWA
8	tabletop	ahead	self-assured

35-C. Take a 1-minute timing on the first paragraph to establish your base speed. Then take several 1-minute timings on the remaining paragraphs. As soon as you equal or exceed your base speed on one paragraph, advance to the next one. All lines should end evenly at the right margin.

35-C. SUSTAINED TYPING: ROUGH DRAFT

9   Several of our subscribers have reported that they get   12
10 a lot of junk mail these days that publicizes the many get- 24
11 rich schemes awaiting them. A word for the wise: Be wary. 36
12 ¶It is true that fortunes are made by entreprenuers who   12
13 capitalize on an idea and make millions. the excitement of 24
14 such challenges can help fulfill the lives of many persons. 36
15   But it is quite true that three have been thousands of 12
16 aspiring millionairs who have lost sizeable investments. a 24
17 proposal to make other rich should be looked at care fully. 36
18   modern investors are seeking increasingly the service   12
19 of financial consultents. They have regular qualificatoins 24
20 in family financal planning and wieghing invest ment risks. 36

| 1 | 2 | 3 | 4 | 5 | 6 | 7 | 8 | 9 | 10 | 11 | 12 |

31-J. ONE-PAGE REPORT

Type Report 1, using double spacing and making the corrections indicated by the proofreaders' marks. Use the visual guide on Workguide page 59.

REPORT 1

Line: 6 inches (60 pica/70 elite)
Tab: 5, center
Spacing: double
Paper: plain
Workguide: 59

WP Word processing programs allow a block of text (a character, word, sentence, or paragraph) to be automatically inserted (∧) into or deleted (↗) from the existing text.

|↓13

FORMS OF BUSINESS ORGANIZATION 6

A Report for Introduction to Business ↓2 13

By Patti Zhuang ↓2 16

↓3

Nearly every business organization in the United States 28

is owned by an individual or by a group of ∧*private* citizens. Sole 41

proprietorships, partnerships, and corporations are by far 51

the most common ∧*forms of* business ∧*organization* types. 61

↓3

SOLE PROPRIETORSHIPS 65

A sole proprietorship is a business that is owned by one 76

person. this individual receives all of the profits earned 89

by that business but is also (responsible personally) for all 100

of the liabilities incurred. *Sole proprietorships are* This is the most prevalent type 116

of owner ship in the country. 122

PARTNERSHIPS 124

¶ Partnerships are businesses owned and managed by two or more 136

persons. In this type of organization, the profits and re- 148

sponsibilities are shared by all members of the partner ship. 160

Each partner's role is usually described in writing. 171

CORPORATIONS 173

A corporation is the most common form of ownership for 184

larger ∧business firms. In this form of ownership, a *group* bunch of people 198

create a legal entity that assumes all risks and functions 210

independently of the owners. 215

34-E. ONE-PAGE REPORTS

Type Reports 6 and 7. Use double spacing, and make the corrections indicated by the proofreaders' marks. Use Workguide page 59 as a visual guide, and preview the revisions before you begin typing.

REPORT 6
ONE-PAGE REPORT

Line: 6 inches
Spacing: double
Paper: plain
Workguide: 59

Using proofreaders' marks to edit and revise a document prior to producing the final copy is called *editing*.

REPORT 7
Retype Report 6, but add the subtitle *A Report for Introduction to Business* and two paragraph headings: *Home Insurance* before the third paragraph and *Auto Insurance* before the fourth paragraph.

TYPES OF INSURANCE   4

By Patti Zhuang   7

All of us are exposed to a variety of risks every day.   18

Insurance is designed to provide protection against ordinary   30

risks. Among the many kinds of available insurance, the fol-   42

lowing are types of policies held by most people.   52

PROPERTY INSURANCE   55

Property insurance is designed to cover financial losses in-   67

curred by damage or destruction of property. home and auto   79

auto insurance are two examples of this type of coverage.   89

Home insurance covers losses from damage to a home and/or   100

its contents. This could include such things as fire,   111

vandalism, or even lightning.   117

Automobile insurance protects against losses from damage   129

to or by an automobile. Accidents, fire, theft, and   139

liability lawsuits are usual. coverages.   147

HEALTH INSURANCE   150

Health insurance coverage is purchased commonly by business firms for   164

their employees as well as by individuals. possible coverages   177

include hospitalization, dental, optical, and disability   188

insurance. Few people can afford the high cost of medical   200

services today without health insurance protection.   210

Line: 60 spaces
Tab: 5, center
Spacing: single
Drills: 2 times
Workguide: 57–60
Format Guide: 21–22
Tape: 14B

LESSON
32

ONE-PAGE REPORTS

Goals: To type 33 wam/3'/5e; to format one-page reports.

32-A. WARMUP

S 1 Six men met them when the bus jerked to a stop at the gate.
A 2 Jacki Baxter cleverly equipped a dozen white magnetometers.
N 3 Lynn moved from 369 South 42 Street to 508 North 17 Street.

SKILLBUILDING

32-B. Take a 1-minute timing on the first paragraph to establish your base speed. Then take several 1-minute timings on the remaining paragraphs. As soon as you equal or exceed your base speed on one paragraph, advance to the next one.

32-B. SUSTAINED TYPING: SYLLABIC INTENSITY

4   Some young people do not know that the number one goal   12
5 for business is to earn money for the owners. Persons will   24
6 not invest their money if there is little chance of profit.   36

7   When they invest the money, they also provide new jobs   12
8 for workers. These workers can then support themselves and   24
9 their families and not depend on public funds for a living.   36

10   More money quietly flows into the local economy as the   12
11 paychecks of these workers are expended. This enables some   24
12 more people to work, and the work force size keeps growing.   36

13   When people are aware that the profit motive is a most   12
14 important objective for business investors, they are a good   24
15 deal more appreciative of the functions of a business firm.   36

| | | 2 | | 3 | | 4 | | 5 | | 6 | | 7 | | 8 | | 9 | | 10 | | 11 | | 12 |

32-C. DIAGNOSTIC TYPING: ALPHABET

Turn to the Diagnostic Typing: Alphabet routine on pages SB-1–SB-3. Take the Pretest, and record your performance on Workguide page 5. Then practice the drill lines for those reaches on which you made errors.

32-D. Spacing: double. Record your score.

32-D. SKILL MEASUREMENT: 3-MINUTE TIMED WRITING

16   It is natural for a new college graduate to think that   12
17 the perfect job is waiting. Some of my friends have found,   24
18 though, that it might not turn out this way.   33
19   What experience have you had? This is often the first   45
20 question that is asked. And, of course, the young graduate   57
21 is amazed that the degree alone won't do it.   66
22   And if you can't get a job, how do you get experience?   78
23 Some succeed by securing part-time work; others are able to   90
24 get free-lance assignments in related areas.   99

| | | 2 | | 3 | | 4 | | 5 | | 6 | | 7 | | 8 | | 9 | | 10 | | 11 | | 12 |

Line: 60 spaces
Tab: 5, center
Spacing: single
Drills: 2 times
Format Guide: 23–24
Tape: 16A

ONE-PAGE REPORTS

Goals: To type 34 wam/3′/5e; to format reports from rough-draft copy.

34-A. WARMUP

S 1 They said they will not take a jet when they take the trip.
A 2 Jess quit before two lazy men excavated gravel in the park.
N 3 Prices on lots 398 and 621 were raised from 47 to 50 cents.

SKILLBUILDING

34-B. Make two copies. Copy 1: Type each sentence on a separate line. Copy 2: Type each sentence on a separate line, but tab-indent it 5 spaces.

34-B. TECHNIQUE TYPING: RETURN/ENTER KEY

4 Where is the new office? It is located on the fifth floor.
5 Is there sufficient space? Yes, it is a very large office.
6 Will I have my own office? No, room dividers will be used.

7 Three telephone lines are needed. A recorder will be used.
8 New furniture has been ordered. We will install carpeting.
9 Office supplies have been ordered. Storage room is scarce.

10 We will move on December 1. Will a moving company be used?
11 One new person will be employed. What will that person do?
12 We will be in a new building. Are there parking lots near?

34-C. DIAGNOSTIC TYPING: NUMBERS

Turn to the Diagnostic Typing: Numbers routine on pages SB-4–SB-5. Take the Pretest, and record your performance on Workguide page 5. Then practice the drill lines for those reaches on which you made errors.

34-D. Spacing: double. Record your score.

34-D. SKILL MEASUREMENT: 3-MINUTE TIMED WRITING

13   Nonverbal communication gives extra meaning to what we   12
14 say. Posture, hand gestures, and facial expressions convey   24
15 our inner thoughts more accurately than words do.   34
16   One can stress a point with just a nod of the head and   46
17 by a change of expression. Eye contact may signal a person   58
18 that you are listening or you couldn't care less.   68
19   The use of such extras in a formal speech adds zest to   80
20 what may be quite boring. And at times, unknown to the one   92
21 speaking, their power may carry the true message.   102

| | | 2 | 3 | 4 | 5 | 6 | 7 | 8 | 9 | 10 | 11 | 12

32-E. ONE-PAGE REPORTS

Type Reports 2 and 3, using double spacing and making the corrections indicated by the proofreaders' marks. Use the visual guide found on Workguide page 59.

REPORT 2
ONE-PAGE REPORT

Line: 6 inches (60 pica/70 elite)
Tab: 5, center
Spacing: double
Paper: plain
Workguide: 59

You must listen for the bell to end your lines, as some words have been changed.

WP

Input is information that is sent to word processors for processing. Examples of input are longhand, shorthand, and dictation. After the input is typed, changes (called *revisions*) are often made in a document. Only the changed material must be retyped, as the original document is stored on a disk in the word processor.

REPORT 3

Retype Report 2 with these changes:
1. Add the subtitle *A Report for Beginning Typing*.
2. Delete the two paragraph headings.

PARTS OF A REPORT   3

By Susan L. Dixon   7

A class report may contain several special parts in addition to   20

the body of the report. Some of these special additional parts come   31

before the body, and some come after it.   39

INTRODUCTORY PARTS   43

The title page and the table of contents are part s of a   54

report that come before the main body.   61

Title Page. The title page is the cover page for a long   72

report. It identifies the author, title, and date of the   84

report. The number and name of the course for which the re-   95

port is being prepared should also be shown.   104

Table of contents. The table of contents lists the main sec-   116

tions and the pages on which each of these sections begins.   128

It is not required for a report of only a few pages.   139

Bibliography   141

The bibliography comes at the end of the report. It   152

lists all the journals, books, and other sources that the   163

writer used to prepare the report. With this listing, the   175

reader is able to study refer to the same publications for additional   188

informatoin. There fore, there should be enough information   197

should be provided so that the reader can locate a particular source in   211

the library.   214

33-E.   FORMATTING ENUMERATIONS

Read the information in Report 4 before you type the assignments in this section. Study the format so that you get a mental picture of the layout before you begin typing.

↓13

ENUMERATIONS

↓3

2

REPORT 4
ENUMERATION

Line: 6 inches (60 pica/70 elite)
Tab: 4
Spacing: single
Paper: plain

WP   Many software programs have a tab indent feature or temporary left margin that allows the operator to use word wrap on enumerations.

1.   An enumeration may be any series of numbered items. How-   14
     ever, to most people the word means a displayed listing   26
     like this one, with the numbers standing out at the left.   37
                                                             ↓2
2.   The numbers are typed at the left margin and are followed   49
     by a period and 2 spaces. To align the turnover lines of   61
     copy, a tab stop is set 4 spaces in from the left margin.   72

3.   Items are single-spaced without any blank lines between   84
     them if most items take one line or less. However, if   95
     most items require more than one line (as in this   105
     enumeration), they are single-spaced with 1 blank line   116
     between items.   119

4.   The periods following the numbers should be vertically   131
     aligned. If the enumeration runs to ten or more items,   142
     the left margin must be reset 1 space to the left.   152

↓13

CITY OF ST. CLOUD

↓3

3

REPORT 5
OUTLINE

Line: block center horizontally
Tab: 4, 8
Spacing: single
Paper: plain

WP   Some software programs contain an outlining feature that automatically formats different levels of headings and allows the operator to rearrange headings easily.

Use the margin release lever to backspace for roman numerals II and III. The periods will then align vertically.

```
  I.  ADMINISTRATIVE OFFICES                              9
                        ↓2
      A.  City Manager                                   12
      B.  Finance and Accounting                         17
      C.  City Clerk                                     20
                    ↓3
 II.  SERVICE DEPARTMENTS                                25

      A.  Fire Department                                28
      B.  Parks and Recreation Department                35
          1.  Indoor sports facilities                  41
          2.  Outdoor sports facilities                 47
          3.  Parks and marinas                         51
      C.  Police Department                              55

III.  UTILITIES OFFICES                                  60

      A.  Board of Light and Power                       65
      B.  Sewage Disposal Plant                          70
      C.  Water and Street Department                    77
```

Line: 60 spaces
Tab: 5, center
Spacing: single
Drills: 2 times
Format Guide: 21–24
Tape: 15B

LESSON 33

ENUMERATIONS

Goals: To improve speed and accuracy; to improve proofreading skills; to format enumerations.

33-A. WARMUP

S 1 Both girls wore yellow formal gowns to the prom last night.
A 2 Max quickly amazed Joan Bishop with five magic card tricks.
N 3 New inventory counts were 370 as compared with 425 in 1986.

SKILLBUILDING

33-B. Type the exercise and correct all errors.

33-B. PRODUCTION PRACTICE: PROOFREADING

4 　　Do you enjoy expensive paintings but can not afford
5 the huge sums of money required for thier purchase. Just
6 as one might rent a cadillac for a special trip, it is
7 possible to have an expensive painting in your home.
8 While policies do vary, 60-day rentals commonly are priced
9 at approximatley ten per cent of the retail price.
10 　　Art museums throughout the country have adopted
11 this marketing strategy. if the renter decides to buy
12 the painting, the rental price is commonly applied to
13 the purchase price. As you would expect, your credit
14 histry and your character must be verified in advanse.

33-C. Center each line: Tab to center, backspace once for every 2 strokes, and then type the entry. Use double spacing.
　Check: The letter o aligns vertically.

33-C. HORIZONTAL-CENTERING PRACTICE

15 　Roy S. Foreman
16 　Edward A. Rodenberger
17 　Fern Stoddard
18 　Kim M. Roberts
19 　Kevin L. Kronschnabel
20 　B. J. Cloutier
21 　Carolyn Soderman
22 　David Olsen

33-D. PACED PRACTICE

Turn to the Paced Practice routine at the back of the book. Take several 2-minute timings, starting at the point where you left off the last time. Record your progress on Workguide page 6.

56 wam   Going to work has always been a major part of being an
adult. Of course, many adolescents also have jobs that can
keep them extremely busy. The work one does or the job one
holds is a critical factor in determining many other things
about the way a person is able to live.

Various work habits are as crucial to one's success as
the actual job skills and knowledge that one brings to that
job. If one is dependable, organized, accurate, efficient,
cooperative, enthusiastic, and understanding, one should be
quickly recognized by most supervisors.

58 wam   Being dependable is a desirable trait to have. When a
worker says that something will be done by a specific time,
it is quite assuring to a manager to know that a dependable
worker is assigned to it. Workers who are dependable learn
to utilize their time to achieve maximum results.

This trait can also be evident with workers who have a
good record for attendance. If a firm is to be productive,
it is essential to have workers on the job. Of course, the
dependable employee not only is on the job, but also is the
worker who can be counted on to be there on time.

60 wam   Organization is another trait that can be described as
necessary to exhibiting good work habits. To be organized,
a worker should have a sense of being able to plan the work
that is to be done and then to work that plan. It is quite
common to notice that competent workers are well organized.

If an office worker is organized, requests are handled
promptly, correspondence is answered quickly, and paperwork
does not accumulate on the desk. In addition, an organized
office worker returns all telephone calls without delay and
makes a list of things to be accomplished on a daily basis.

DIAGNOSTIC TYPING: ALPHABET

Line: 60 spaces
Spacing: single

The Diagnostic Typing: Alphabet program is designed to diagnose and then correct your keystroking errors. You may use this program at any time after completing Lesson 10 in the text.

Directions

1. Type the Pretest/Posttest passage once, proofread it, and circle errors.
2. In the error chart on Workguide page 5, write the date, the number of errors you made on each key, and your total number of errors. For example, if you typed *rhe* for *the*, that would count as 1 error on the letter *t*.
3. For any letter on which you made 2 or more errors, select the corresponding drill lines and type them twice. If you made only 1 error, type the drill once.
4. If you made no errors on the Pretest/Posttest passage, turn to the practice on troublesome pairs on page SB-3 and type each line once. This section provides intensive practice on those pairs of keys which are most commonly confused.
5. Finally, retype the Pretest/Posttest, and compare your performance with your Pretest.

PRETEST/POSTTEST

Jacob and Zeke Koufax quietly enjoyed jazz music on my
new jukebox. My six or seven pieces of exquisite equipment
helped make their musical selections sound great. I picked
five very quaint waltzes from Gregg Ward's jazz recordings.

PRACTICE: INDIVIDUAL REACHES

aa Isaac badge carry dared eager faced gains habit dials AA
aa jaunt kayak label mamma Nancy oasis paint Qatar rapid AA
aa safer taken guard vague waves exact yacht Zaire Aaron AA

bb about ebbed ebony rugby fiber elbow amber unbar oboes BB
bb arbor cubic oxbow maybe abate abbot debit libel album BB
bb embed obeys urban tubes Sybil above lobby webby bribe BB

cc acted occur recap icing ulcer emcee uncle ocean force CC
cc scale itchy bucks excel Joyce acute yucca decal micro CC
cc mulch McCoy incur octet birch scrub latch couch cycle CC

dd admit daddy edict Magda ideal older index oddly order DD
dd outdo udder crowd Floyd adapt added Edith Idaho folds DD
dd under modem sword misdo fudge rowdy Lydia adept buddy DD

ee aegis beach cents dense eerie fence germs hence piece EE
ee jewel keyed leads media nerve poems penny reach seize EE
ee teach guest verse Wendy Xerox years zesty aerie begin EE

50 wam   We all want to work in a pleasant environment where we
are surrounded with jovial people who never make a mistake.
The realities of the real world tell us, however, that this
likely will not happen; the use of corrective action may be
required.

        For the very reason that this trait is so difficult to
cultivate, all of us should strive to improve the manner in
which we accept constructive criticism. By recognizing the
positive intent of supervisors, each of us can accrue extra
benefits.

52 wam   The worker and the firm might be compared in some ways
with a child and the family unit. Just as a child at times
disagrees with a parent, the worker might question policies
of the company. In each case, there must be procedures for
conflict resolution.

        One option for a vexed child is to run away from home;
an employee may type a letter of resignation. A far better
option in both situations is the discussion of differences.
The child remains loyal to family, and the employee remains
loyal to the company.

54 wam   The person who aspires to a role in management must be
equal to the challenge. Those who have supervisory respon-
sibilities must make fine judgments as decisions are formed
that affect the entire organization. The challenge of managing is difficult and lonely.

        While other labels are sometimes used to explain basic
functions of management, the concepts remain the same. The
four main functions are involved with planning, organizing,
actuating, and controlling of such components as personnel,
production, and sales of goods.

```
ff after defer offer jiffy gulfs infer often dwarf cuffs FF
ff awful afoul refer affix edify Wolfe infra aloof scarf FF
ff bluff afoot defer daffy fifty sulfa softy surfs stuff FF

gg again edges egged soggy igloo Elgin angel ogled Marge GG
gg outgo auger pygmy agaze Edgar Egypt buggy light bulge GG
gg singe doggy organ fugle agree hedge began baggy Niger GG

hh ahead abhor chili Nehru ghost Elihu khaki Lhasa unhat HH
hh aloha phony myrrh shale Ethan while yahoo choir jehad HH
hh ghoul Khmer Delhi Ohara photo rhino shake think while HH

ii aired bides cider dices eight fifth vigil highs radii II
ii jiffy kinds lives mired niece oiled piped rigid siren II
ii tired build visit wider exist yield aimed binds cigar II

jj major eject fjord Ouija enjoy Cajun Fijis Benjy bijou JJ
jj banjo jabot jacks jaded jails Japan jaunt jazzy jeans JJ
jj jeeps jeers jelly jerks jibed jiffy jilts joint joker JJ

kk Akron locks vodka peeks mikes sulky links okras larks KK
kk skins Yukon hawks tykes makes socks seeks hiker sulks KK
kk tanks Tokyo jerky pesky nukes gawks maker ducks cheek KK

ll alarm blame clank idled elope flame glows Chloe Iliak LL
ll ankle Lloyd inlet olive plane burly sleet atlas Tulsa LL
ll yowls axles nylon alone blunt claim idler elite flute LL

mm among adman demit pigmy times calms comma unman omits MM
mm armor smell umber axmen lymph gizmo amass admit demon MM
mm dogma imply films mommy omits armed smear bumpy axman MM

nn ankle Abner envoy gnome Johns input knife kilns hymns NN
nn Donna onion apnea Arnes snore undid owned cynic angle NN
nn entry gnash inset knoll nanny onset barns sneer unfit NN

oo aorta bolts coats dolls peony fouls goofs hoped iotas OO
oo jolts kooky loins moral noise poled Roger soaks total OO
oo quote voter would Saxon yo-yo zones bombs colts doles OO

pp apple epoch flips alpha ample input droop puppy sharp PP
pp spunk soups expel typed April Epsom slips helps empty PP
pp unpin optic peppy corps spite upset types apply creep PP

qq Iraqi equal pique roque squad tuque aquae equip toque QQ
qq squab squat squak squaw quail qualm quart queen quell QQ
qq query quest quick quiet quilt quirk quota quote quoth QQ

rr array bring crave drive erode freak grain three irate RR
rr kraft inrun orate Barry tramp urges livre wrote lyric RR
rr Ezars armor broth crown drawl erect freer grade throw RR
```

42 wam
Newly employed workers are quite often judged by their
skills in informal verbal situations. A simple exchange of
greetings when being introduced to a customer is an example
that illustrates one situation.

A new employee might have a very good idea at a small-
group meeting. However, unless that idea can be verbalized
to the other members in a clear, concise manner, they won't
develop a proper appreciation.

44 wam
Many supervisors state that they want their workers to
use what they refer to as common sense. Common sense tells
a person to answer the phone, to open the mail, and to lock
the door at the end of the working day.

It is easy to see that this trait equates with the use
of good judgment. The prize employee will want to capitalize on each new experience that will help him or her to use
better judgments when making decisions.

46 wam
Every person should set as a goal the proper balancing
of the principal components in one's life. Few people will
disagree with the belief that the family is the most important of the four main ingredients in a human life.

Experts in the career education field are quick to say
that family must be joined with leisure time, vocation, and
citizenship in order to encompass one's full "career." The
right balance results in satisfaction and success.

48 wam
As we become an information society, there is an ever-
increasing awareness of office costs. Such costs are labor
intensive, and those who must justify them are increasingly
concerned about workers' use of time management principles.

Researchers in the time management area have developed
several techniques for examining office tasks and analyzing
routines. The realization that "time is money" is only the
beginning and must be followed with an educational program.

```
ss ashen bombs specs binds bares leafs bangs sighs issue SS
ss necks mills teams turns solos stops stirs dress diets SS
ss usury Slavs stows abyss asked stabs cords mares beefs SS

tt attic debts pacts width Ethel often eight itchy alter TT
tt until motto optic earth stops petty couth newts extra TT
tt myths Aztec atone doubt facts veldt ether sight Italy TT

uu audio bumps cured dumps deuce fuels gulps huffy opium UU
uu junta kudos lulls mumps nudge outdo purer ruler super UU
uu tulip revue exult yucca azure auger burns curve duels UU

vv avows event ivory elves envoy overt larva mauve savvy VV
vv avant every rivet Elvis anvil coves curvy divvy avert VV
vv evict given valve ovens serve paves evade wives hover VV

ww awash bwana dwarf brews Gwenn schwa kiwis Elwin unwed WW
ww owner Irwin sweet twins byway awake dwell pewee tower WW
ww Erwin swims twirl awful dwelt Dewey owlet swamp twine WW

xx axiom exile fixed Bronx toxin Sioux Exxon pyxie axman XX
xx exert fixes Leonx oxbow beaux calyx maxim exact sixth XX
xx proxy taxes excel mixed boxer axing Texas sixty epoxy XX

yy maybe bylaw cynic dying eying unify gypsy hypos Benjy YY
yy Tokyo hilly rummy Ronny loyal pygmy diary Syria types YY
yy buyer vying Wyatt epoxy crazy kayak Byram cycle bawdy YY

zz Azure Czech adzes bezel dizzy Franz froze Liszt ritzy ZZ
zz abuzz tizzy hazed czars maize Ginza oozes blitz fuzzy ZZ
zz jazzy mazes mezzo sized woozy Hertz dizzy Hazel Gomez ZZ
```

PRACTICE: TROUBLESOME PAIRS

A/S Sal said he asked Sara Ash for a sample of the raisins.
B/V Beverly believes Bob behaved very bravely in Beaverton.
C/D Clyde and Dick decided they could decode an old decree.

E/W We wondered whether Andrew waited for Walter and Wendy.
F/G Griffin goofed in figuring their gifted golfer's score.
H/J Joseph joshed with Judith when John jogged to Johnetta.

I/O A novice violinist spoiled Orville Olin's piccolo solo.
K/L Kelly, unlike Blake, liked to walk as quickly as Karla.
M/N Many women managed to move among the mounds of masonry.

O/P A pollster polled a population in Phoenix by telephone.
Q/A Quincy acquired one quality quartz ring at the banquet.
R/T Three skaters traded their tartan trench coats to Bart.

U/Y Buy your supply of gifts during your busy July journey.
X/C The exemptions exceed the expert's wildest expectation.
Z/A Eliza gazed as four lazy zebra zigzagged near a gazebo.

32 wam   Whichever career path is selected, the degree of pride shown in one's work has to be at a high level. Others will judge you by how well you do your work.

Your self-image is affected by what you believe others think of you as well as by what you think of yourself. The quality of your efforts impacts on both.

34 wam   If a matter is important to a supervisor or to a firm, it should be important to the worker. The responsible person can be depended on to put priorities in order.

The higher your job-satisfaction level, the greater is the likelihood that you will be pleased with all aspects of your life. Positive attitudes will bring rewards.

36 wam   Whenever people work together, attention must be given to the human relations factor. A quality organization will concern itself with interactional skills needed by workers.

Respect, courtesy, and patience are examples of just a few of the words that combine to bring about positive human relationships in the office as well as in other situations.

38 wam   The alarm didn't go off. The bus was late. The baby-sitter is sick. The car wouldn't start. And for some, the list of excuses goes on. Be thankful that this list is not like yours.

You will keep the tardy times to a minimum by planning and anticipating. And you will realize that those who jump the gun by quitting work early at the end of the day have a bad habit.

40 wam   Some people take forever to become acquainted with the office routines. Some must have every task explained along with a list of things to be done. Some go ahead and search for new things to do.

Initiative is a trait that managers look for in people who are promoted while on the job. A prized promotion with a nice pay raise can be the reward for demonstrating that a person has new ideas.

DIAGNOSTIC TYPING: NUMBERS

Line: 60 spaces
Spacing: single

The Diagnostic Typing: Numbers program is designed to diagnose and then correct your keystroking errors. You may use this program at any time after completing Lesson 20 in the text.

Directions

1. Type the Pretest/Posttest passage once, proofread it, and circle errors.
2. In the error chart on Workguide page 5, write the date, the number of errors you made on each key, and your total number of errors. For example, if you typed *24* for *25*, that would count as 1 error on the number *5*.
3. For any number on which you made 2 or more errors, select the corresponding drill lines and type them twice. If you made only 1 error, type the drill once.
4. Make one copy of the drills on page SB-5 that contain all the numbers. (If you made no errors on the Pretest/Posttest passage, type the drills that contain all the numbers, repeat, and then repeat again as you strive to reach new speed levels.)
5. Finally, retype the Pretest/Posttest, and compare your performance with your Pretest.

PRETEST/POSTTEST

My inventory records dated December 31, 1989, revealed we had 458 pints, 2,069 quarts, and 4,774 gallons of paint. We had 2,053 brushes, 568 scrapers, 12,063 wallpaper rolls, 897 knives, 5,692 mixers, 480 ladders, and 371 step stools.

PRACTICE: INDIVIDUAL REACHES

1 aq aq1 aq1qa 111 ants 101 aunts 131 apples 171 animals a1
They got 11 answers correct for the 11 questions in BE 121.
Those 11 adults loaded the 711 animals between 1 and 2 p.m.
All 111 agreed that 21 of those 31 are worthy of the honor.

2 sw sw2 sw2ws 222 sets 242 steps 226 salads 252 saddles s2
The 272 summer tourists saw the 22 soldiers and 32 sailors.
Your September 2 date was all right for 292 of 322 persons.
The 22 surgeons said 221 of those 225 operations went well.

3 de de3 de3ed 333 dots 303 drops 313 demons 393 dollars d3
Bus 333 departed at 3 p.m. with the 43 dentists and 5 boys.
She left 33 dolls and 73 decoys at 353 West Addison Street.
The 13 doctors helped some of the 33 druggists in Room 336.

4 fr fr4 fr4rf 444 fans 844 farms 444 fishes 644 fiddles f4
My 44 friends bought 84 farms and sold over 144 franchises.
She sold 44 fish and 440 beef dinners for $9.40 per dinner.
The '54 Ford had only 40,434 fairly smooth miles by July 4.

20 wam   Spending time on a job is work. For most people, work
is something they have to do to survive.

        Today, work means more than staying alive. People ex-
pect different rewards from their jobs.

22 wam   Work can be interesting, and more and more workers are
now saying that their work should be interesting.

        Sure, there are many boring jobs, and every job always
has some less exciting and more routine features.

24 wam   Today there are many different types of jobs which you
may choose from which range from the routine to the exotic.

        If you begin your planning early, you can work at dif-
ferent types of jobs and learn from the experience of each.

26 wam   Workers tend to identify with their careers, and their
careers in a real sense give them a sense of importance and
belonging.

        People's jobs also help determine how they spend their
spare time, who their friends are, and sometimes even where
they live.

28 wam   Work can take place in school, in a factory or office,
at home, or outside; it can be done for money or experience
or even voluntarily.

        It should be quite clear that work can be any activity
that involves a type of responsibility. The same thing can
be said about a job.

30 wam   A career relates to work that is done for pay. But it
means more than a particular job; it is the pattern of work
done throughout your lifetime.

        A career suggests looking ahead, planning, and setting
goals and reaching them. The well-planned career becomes a
part of the individual's life.

5 fr fr5 fr5rf 555 furs 655 foxes 555 flares 455 fingers f5
They now own 155 restaurants, 45 food stores, and 55 farms.
They ordered 45, 55, 65, and 57 yards of that new material.
Flight 855 flew over Farmington at 5:50 p.m. on December 5.

6 jy jy6 jy6yj 666 jets 266 jeeps 666 jewels 866 jaguars j6
Purchase orders numbered 6667 and 6668 were sent yesterday.
Those 66 jazz players played for 46 juveniles in Room 6966.
The 6 judges reviewed the 66 journals on November 16 or 26.

7 ju ju7 ju7uj 777 jays 377 jokes 777 joists 577 juniors j7
The 17 jets carried 977 jocular passengers above 77 cities.
Those 277 jumping beans went to 77 junior scouts on May 17.
The 7 jockeys rode 77 jumpy horses between March 17 and 27.

8 ki ki8 ki8ik 888 keys 488 kites 888 knives 788 kittens k8
My 8 kennels housed 83 dogs, 28 kids, and 88 other animals.
The 18 kind ladies tied 88 knots in the 880 pieces of rope.
The 8 men saw 88 kelp bass, 38 kingfish, and 98 king crabs.

9 lo lo9 lo9ol 999 lads 599 larks 999 ladies 699 leaders 19
All 999 leaves fell from the 9 large oaks at 389 Largemont.
The 99 linemen put 399 large rolls of tape on for 19 games.
Those 99 lawyers put 899 legal-size sheets in the 19 limos.

0 ;p ;p0 ;p0p; 100 pens 900 pages 200 pandas 800 pencils ;0
There were 1,000 people who lived in the 300 private homes.
The 10 party stores are open from 1:00 p.m. until 9:00 p.m.
They edited 500 pages in 1 book and 1,000 pages in 2 books.

All numbers   ala s2s d3d f4f f5f j6j j7j k8k 191 ;0; Add 5 and 9 and 16.
Those 67 jumpsuits were shipped to 238 Birch on October 14.
Invoices numbered 294 and 307 are to be paid by November 5.
Flight 674 is scheduled to leave from Gate 18 at 11:35 a.m.

All numbers   ala s2s d3d f4f f5f j6j j7j k8k 191 ;0; Add 6 and 8 and 29.
That 349-page script called for 18 actors and 20 actresses.
The check for $50 was sent to 705 Garfield Street, not 507.
The 14 researchers asked the 469 Californians 23 questions.

All numbers   ala s2s d3d f4f f5f j6j j7j k8k 191 ;0; Add 3 and 4 and 70.
They built 1,200 houses on the 345-acre site by the canyon.
Her research showed that gold was at 397 in September 1986.
For $868 extra, they bought 27 new books and 62 used books.

All numbers   ala s2s d3d f4f f5f j6j j7j k8k 191 ;0; Add 5 and 7 and 68.
A bank auditor arrived on May 26, 1988, and left on May 30.
The 4 owners open the stores from 9:30 a.m. until 6:00 p.m.
After 1,374 miles on the bus, she must then drive 125 more.

PACED PRACTICE

Line: 60 spaces
Spacing: single

The Paced Practice skillbuilding program builds speed and accuracy in short, easy steps, using individualized goals and immediate feedback. You may use this program at any time after completing Lesson 10 in the text.

This section contains a series of 2-minute timings for speeds ranging from 12 wam to 60 wam. The first time you use these timings, select a passage that is 2 wam higher than your current typing speed. Use this two-stage practice pattern to achieve each speed goal—first concentrate on speed, and then work on accuracy.

Have someone call out each ¼-minute interval as you type. Strive to be at the appropriate point in the passage marked by a small superior number as each ¼-minute interval is announced—typing neither too fast nor too slowly.

Speed Goal. Take successive timings on the same passage until you can complete it in 2 minutes without regard to errors.

When you have achieved your speed goal, record the date on the Progress Record on Workguide page 6. For example, if your speed goal was 28 wam, record the date beside *28s* (for *speed*). Then work on accuracy.

Accuracy Goal. To type accurately, you need to slow down—just a bit. Therefore, to reach your accuracy goal, drop back 2 wam to the previous passage. Take successive timings on this passage until you can complete it in 2 minutes with no more than 2 errors. When you have achieved your accuracy goal, record the date on the Progress Record.

For example, if you achieved your earlier speed goal of 28 wam, you would work on 26 wam for accuracy and record the date you achieved your goal beside *26a* (for *accuracy*). Then you would move up 4 wam (for example, to the 30-wam passage) and work for speed again.

12 wam
What is the meaning of work? Why do most people work?
The concept of work and careers is of interest to you.

14 wam
When doing something that is required, you think of it
as working.
When doing something that you want to do, you think of
it as fun.

16 wam
We often do not consider the amount of time and effort
spent doing a task.
If we did, we would realize that many people work hard
even while playing.

18 wam
For example, people sweat, strain, or even suffer dis-
comfort when playing a sport.
They do this for fun. If they were required to do it,
they might not be so willing.

PROGRESSIVE PRACTICE: ALPHABET

Line: 60 spaces
Spacing: single

This skillbuilding routine contains a series of 30-second timings that range from 16 wam to 68 wam. The first time you use these timings, select a passage that is 2 words a minute higher than your current speed. Take repeated timings on the passage until you can complete it within 30 seconds with no errors. When you have achieved your goal, record the date on the Progress Record on Workguide page 5. Then move on to the next passage and repeat the procedure.

16 wam   An author is the creator of a document.

18 wam   Access means to call up data out of storage.

20 wam   A byte represents one character to your computer.

22 wam   To store means to insert data in memory for later use.

24 wam   Soft copy is text that is displayed on your display screen.

26 wam   Memory is the part of a word processor that stores information.

28 wam   A menu is a list of choices to guide the operator through a function.

30 wam   A sheet feeder is a device that will insert sheets of paper into a printer.

32 wam   Boilerplate copy is a reusable passage that is stored until needed in a program.

34 wam   Downtime is the length of time that equipment is not usable because of a malfunction.

36 wam   To execute means to perform an action specified by an operator or by a computer program.

38 wam   Output is the result of a word processing operation. It is in either printed or magnetic form.

40 wam   Format refers to the physical features which affect the appearance and arrangement of a document.

42 wam My 7 or 8 buyers ordered 7 dozen in sizes 5 and 6 after the 14 to 32 percent discounts had been granted.

44 wam There were 34 women and 121 men waiting in line at the gate for the 65 to 87 tickets to the sold-out concert.

46 wam Steve had listed 5 or 6 items on Purchase Order 241 when he saw that Purchase Requisition 87 contained 3 or 4 more.

48 wam The item numbered 278 will sell for about 90 percent of the value of the 16 items that have a code number shown as 435.

50 wam The manager stated that 98 of the 750 randomly selected new valves had about 264 defects, far in excess of the usual 31 norm.

52 wam Half of the 625 volunteers received about 90 percent of the charity pledges. Approximately 83 of the 147 agencies will get funds.

54 wam Merico hired 94 part-time workers to help the 378 full-time employees during that 62-day period when sales go up by 150 percent or more.

56 wam Kaye only hit 1 for 6 in the first 29 games after an 8-game streak in which she batted 0 for 4. She then hit at a .573 average for 3 games.

58 wam The mailman delivered 98 letters during the week to 734 Oak Street and also delivered 52 letters to 610 Pioneer Road as he returned on Route 58.

60 wam Pat said that about 1 of 5 of the 379 swimmers had a chance of being among the top 20. The finest 6 of those 48 divers will receive about 16 awards.

62 wam It rained from 3 to 6 inches, and 18 of the 21 farmers were fearful that 4 to 7 inches more would flood about 950 acres along 3 miles of the new Route 78.

64 wam The 7 sacks weighed 48 pounds, more than the 30 pounds that I had thought. All 24 think the 92-pound bag is at least 6 or 9 or 15 pounds beyond what it weighs.

66 wam They ordered 7 of those 8 options for 54 of the 63 vehicles last month. They now own over 120 dump trucks for use in 9 of the 15 regions in the new 20-county area.

68 wam Andrew was 8 or 9 years old when they moved to 632 Glendale Street from the 1700 block of Horseshoe Lane about 45 miles directly southwest of Boca Raton, Florida 33434.

42 wam   A font is a set of type of one size or style which includes all letters, numbers, and punctuation marks.

44 wam   Ergonomics is the science of adapting working conditions or equipment to meet most physical needs of workers.

46 wam   Home position is the starting position of a document; it is typically the upper left corner of the display screen.

48 wam   An electronic typewriter is a word processor which has only limited functions; it typically does not include a display.

50 wam   An optical scanner is a device that can read text and enter it into a word processor without the need to rekeyboard the data.

52 wam   Hardware refers to the physical equipment used, such as the central processing unit, display screen, keyboard, printer, or drive.

54 wam   A peripheral device is any piece of equipment that will extend the capabilities of a system but that is not necessary for operation.

56 wam   A split screen displays two or more different images at the same time; it can, for example, display two different pages of a legal document.

58 wam   A daisy wheel is a printing element that is made of plastic or metal and is used on different printers. Each character is at the end of a spoke.

60 wam   A cursor is a special character, often a blinking box or an underscore, which shows where the next typed character will appear on the display screen.

62 wam   The hot zone is the area before the right margin, typically five to ten characters wide, where words may have to be divided or transferred to a new line.

64 wam   Turnaround time is the length of time needed for a document to be keyboarded, edited, proofread, corrected if required, printed, and returned to the executive.

66 wam   A local area network is a system that uses cable or another means to allow high-speed communication among various kinds of electronic equipment within a small area.

68 wam   To search and replace means to direct the word processor to locate a character, word, or group of words wherever it occurs in the document and replace it with new text.

PROGRESSIVE PRACTICE: NUMBERS

Line: 60 spaces
Spacing: single

This skillbuilding routine contains a series of 30-second timings that range from 16 wam to 68 wam. The first time you use these timings, select a passage that is 4 to 6 words a minute *lower* than your current alphabetic speed. (The reason for selecting a lower speed goal is that sentences with numbers are more difficult to type.) Take repeated timings on the passage until you can complete it within 30 seconds with no errors. When you have achieved your goal, record the date on the Progress Record on Workguide page 5. Then move on to the next passage and repeat the procedure.

16 wam   There were now 21 children in Room 211.

18 wam   Fewer than 12 of the 121 boxes have arrived.

20 wam   Maybe 2 of the 21 applicants met all 12 criteria.

22 wam   There were 34 letters addressed to 434 West Cranbrook.

24 wam   Jan reported that there were 434 freshmen and 43 transfers.

26 wam   The principal assigned 3 of those 4 students to Room 343 at
          noon.

28 wam   Only 1 or 2 of the 34 latest invoices were more than 1 page
          in length.

30 wam   They met 11 of the 12 players who received awards from 3 of
          the 4 coaches.

32 wam   Those 5 vans carried 46 passengers on the first trip and 65
          on the next 3 trips.

34 wam   We first saw 3 and then 4 beautiful eagles on Route 65 at 5
          a.m. on Monday, June 12.

36 wam   The 6 companies produced 51 of the 62 records that received
          awards for 3 of 4 categories.

38 wam   The 12 trucks hauled the 87 cows and 65 horses to the farm,
          which was about 21 miles northeast.

40 wam   She moved from 87 Bayview Drive to 657 Cole Street and then
          3 blocks south to 412 Gulbranson Avenue.